Mary Ratcliffe

Englisch: Rechtschreibung, Diktate und Wortschatz üben 7. Schuljahr

MANZ VERLAG

Manz Verlag

Lektorat: Harald Kotlarz, Rottenburg
Herstellung: S · M · P Oehler, Remseck
Umschlaggestaltung: Zembsch' Werkstatt, München
Illustration: Sven Palmowski, Stuttgart
Satz: S · M · P Oehler, Remseck
Druck: Ludwig Auer GmbH, Donauwörth
Printed in Germany

ISBN 3-7863-2102-7

Tipps zum Training mit diesem Buch

In diesem Buch kannst du Wörter üben, die du im Laufe des 7. Schuljahres kennen lernen wirst, aber auch einige schwierige der letzten beiden Jahre wiederholen. Praktisch alle diese Wörter findest du auch in deinem Lehrbuch, es werden dir also kaum neue Wörter begegnen.

Das Buch besteht aus zwei großen Blöcken (BCD und EFG). Jeder Block behandelt den Wortschatz, den du in einem Halbjahr neu lernen wirst. Es empfiehlt sich also, erst gegen Weihnachten den ersten Teil zu trainieren und gegen Oster dann den zweiten.

Jeder Block besteht aus drei Kapiteln. Im Kapitel ***Words in context*** kannst du dir die Wörter einzeln und in einem sinnvollen Zusammenhang einprägen. Übungen und Rätsel helfen dir dabei. Hier kannst du zum Beispiel ähnlich oder gleich klingende Wörter, die aber unterschiedlich geschrieben werden, üben. Und du lernst auch, über den Sinnzusammenhang die richtige Schreibweise zu verwenden.

Im ***Word workshop*** („Wörter-Werkstatt") werden die Lernwörter so angeordnet, dass du bestimmte Besonderheiten, wie Groß- und Kleinschreibung, stumme Buchstaben, Pluralformen oder unbetonte Silben, gründlich üben kannst.

Jeder Block endet mit einer großen Auswahl an **Diktaten**, in denen die Kenntnisse getestet werden können. Natürlich kannst du auch wahlweise mit den Diktaten anfangen. Du solltest dir dann deine Fehler notieren und die entsprechenden Teile im Übungsangebot trainieren. Du findest eine genaue Übersicht dazu auf den Seiten 5 und 6.

Keine Angst vor der **Lautschrift**! Im Kapitel A wird sie dir gezeigt und du kannst sie in einigen lustigen Übungen gleich selbst anwenden. Sie ist hilfreich – und notwendig – damit beim Vorlesen die Wörter auch richtig ausgesprochen werden. Dabei kommt es besonders auf die kleinen Unterschiede an! Du brauchst sie aber auch, um einige Übungen zu bearbeiten.

Wenn du mit einer Übung fertig bist, dann schau in den **Lösungen** nach, ob du alles richtig gemacht hast. Vorher sollstest du aber die **Tipps** durchlesen. Sie helfen dir, auf die richtige Spur zu kommen oder deine Ergebnisse selbst zu überprüfen.

Jetzt blättere das Buch einfach einmal durch. Welches Kapitel spricht dich am meisten an, oder was solltest du für das nächste Diktat sicher beherrschen? Stelle dir dann deinen Trainingsplan zusammen – und auf geht's!

Inhalt

Das Übungsangebot

Der Buchstabe gibt das Kapitel an und die Ziffer die Nummer der Übung.

3. Person Singular -s	**C**11-13, **D**4-5, **F**1-5, **G**1-6
Adjektive / Adverbien	**C**22-26, **D**7-8, **E**2, **F**14-18, **G**14-16
Apostroph	**C**27-30, **D**9-11, **F**19, 21, **G**17-18
Betonung	**B**25, 42, 49, **E**1, 36, **F**32
Doppel- / Einzelkonsonanten	**C**45, **D**21-22, **E**30, **F**23-25
‚False friends'	**B**10, **C**6, 7, **D**23-25, **F**31, **G**23-25
Groß- und Kleinschreibung	**C**31-33, **D**11-12, **F**20, 21, **G**19-22
-ing-Form	**C**14-17, **D**6, **F**10-13, **G**7-13
Pluralformen	**B**13, **C**1-10, **D**1-3, **E**55, **F**1-5, **G**1-6
Konsonanten	**B**4, 5, 18, 28, 52, **C**57-60, **E**10, 17, 59, **F** 29, 33-39
Simple past / past participle	**C**18-21, **D**6, **E**32, 37, 53, **F**6-9, **G**7-11
Stumme Konsonanten	**B**11, 19, 27, 43, 51 **C**54, 62 **D**20, **E**3, 26, **F**26
Unbetonte Silben	**B**12, 26, **C**38-39, 61, **D**16-19, **E**33
Unbetonte Vor- und Nachsilben	**B**35, **C**39-53, **F**40, 41
Vokale	**B**20, 34, 37, 50 **C** 55, 56, 62, **E**59, **F**27- 28
Vokabeltraining	**B**1-3, 8, 9, 17, 24, 32, 33, 40, 41, 48, 57, **C**51, 53, 62, **E**1, 9, 15, 16, 20, 24, 25, 27, 31, 32, 36, 37, 39, 41, 44, 46-49, 52, 57, 62, 63, **G**28-36
Zusammen- und Getrenntschreibung	**C**34-37, **D**13-15, **F**22, **G**21-22
Ähnlich klingende Wörter	**D**25-28, **G**26, 27

Homophone und ähnlich klingende Wortgruppen

a loud – allowed	B55
although – also	E7
bought – board – bored	B7, E13
buy – by	E35
falls – false	B6
here – hear	B31
his – he's	E21
hour – our; hours – ours	E22
its – it's	E18
knows – nose	E29
life – live	B56
made – mate	B22
mouth – mouse	B30
no – know	E61
of – off	E40
passed – past	B53
peace – piece	E6
rode – road	B54
see – sea	E66
side – sight	B14
spend – spent	E11
sun – son	B46
their – there – they're	E28
this – these	E55
through – threw	E45
two – too	B38
where – we're – wear	E12
who – how	E50
whole – hole	B45
your – you're	B15

A Die Lautschrift

Die Vokale

Laut	Deutsches Wort	Englisches Wort
[iː]	s**ie**	gr**ee**n
[i]	**I**dee	German**y**
[ɪ]	d**i**ck	s**i**ster
[e]	F**e**st	t**e**n
[æ]	**ä**lter	bl**a**ck
[ɑː]	D**a**tum	c**ar**d
[ɒ]	s**o**ll	g**o**t
[ɔː]	F**or**m	b**or**ing
[uː]	d**u**	d**o**
[ʊ]	z**u**m	g**oo**d
[ʌ]	s**a**tt	f**u**nny
[ɜː]	Ingeni**eur**	g**ir**l
[ə]	Partn**er**	moth**er**, act**or**

Diese Vokale bilden auch Verbindungen, zum Beispiel:

[ɪə]	h**ie**r	h**ere**
[aʊ]	H**au**s	h**ou**se

Die Konsonanten

Die Lautschrift der meisten Konsonanten ist so, wie im normalen Alphabet, zum Beispiel [t], [h], [p]. Doch auch hier gibt es einige „Geheimzeichen".

Laut	Deutsch	Englisch
[ŋ]	la**ng**	wro**ng**
[ʃ]	**Sch**ule	**sh**e
[tʃ]	Deu**tsch**	**ch**air
[ʒ]	**G**elee	revi**si**on
[dʒ]	**J**ob	**G**erman, **j**ust
[θ]	–	**th**ank you
[ð]	–	**th**at

Wieder andere werden im Englischen anders als im Deutschen ausgesprochen:

[w]	A**u**erhahn	**w**e
[v]	**w**o	se**v**en
[z]	Ha**s**e	plea**s**e, **z**oo

Die Betonung eines Wortes wird mit einem Strich (') **vor** der betonten Silbe angegeben, zum Beispiel: *German* → ['dʒɜ:mən] oder *today* → [tə 'deɪ]

Übungen

1. Unterstreiche das Wort, das in der Lautschrift steht:

a) [tri:] three – tree – free

b) [dʒɒb] shop – job

c) [ʃelf] shelf – self

d) [ʃʊk] joke – shook – shake

e) [zu:] shoe – zoo – so

f) [θru:] through – throw – drew

Schon mal gehört?

Patient: What is wrong with me, Doctor?

Doctor: If you really want to know, you [i:t] too much, you [drɪŋk] too much and you're the ['leɪziɪst] man I've ever known.

Patient: That's fine, Doctor. Can you [træns'leɪt] that into Latin, so that I can have a [wi:k] off [wɜ:k]?

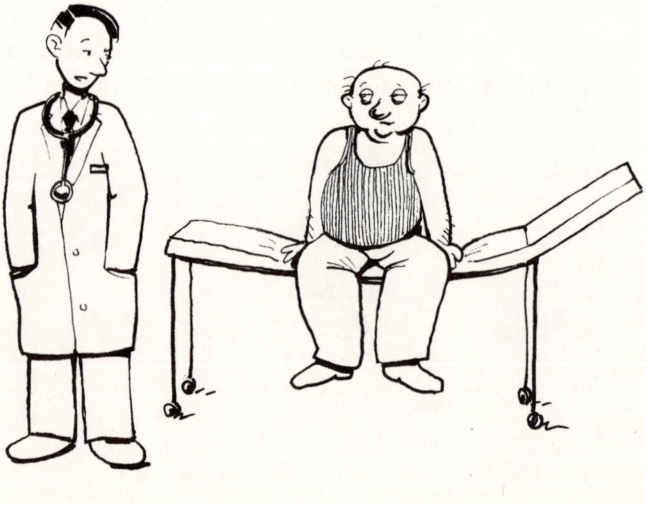

2. Welches Wort steht in der Lautschrift?

a) [ðen] sun – thin – then – than

b) [tʃek] check – shake – Jack

c) [tʃu:z] shoes – choose – chose

d) [faɪv] wave – wife – five

e) [waɪn] fine – wine

f) [ɪ'levn] eleven – elephant

Another [dʒəʊk] for you:
A man was travelling on a country train which was much too [sləʊ]. He got angry and ran to the [frʌnt] of the train.
'Can't you go any ['fɑ:stə], driver?' he asked.
'Yes, sir, I can, but I'm not [ə'laʊd] to [li:v] my train.'

3. Unterstreiche das Wort, das in der Lautschrift steht

a) [fæt] wet – fat – fit

b) [wɒt] vet – foot – what

c) ['ændi] angry – Andy

d) [sʌŋ] sung – sun

e) ['i:zi] easy – easier

f) ['pɑ:ti] partner – party

Some children from the city were visiting a [fɑ:m]. The farmer [ʃəʊd] them a horseshoe.
'Does anybody know what that [mi:nz]?' he asked.
'Of course,' said a little boy. 'It means that one of your horses is ['rʌnɪŋ] around in his [sɒks]!'

4. Finde wieder das Wort in der Lautschrift.

a) [gʊd] good – God – got

b) [ju:] Jew – you – your

c) [drəʊv] drove – drive

d) [faʊnd] find – found – phoned

e) [bɪ'gʌn] begin – began – begun

f) [leɪt] late – light – lit

David's mum made a cake. David found it, still warm, in the ['kɪtʃɪn]. He ate it all up very ['kwɪkli].
His mother came in and saw the ['empti] [pleɪt].
'David! Didn't you think of your ['brʌðə] and sister?' she shouted ['æŋgrɪli].
'Oh yes, all the time,' said David. 'That's [waɪ] I ['hʌrɪd].'

B Words in context 1

The problem page

Mandy und Jane schauen die Zeitschrift Scrapbook an. Jane interessiert sich am meisten für die „problem page".

1. Ergänze den Text mithilfe der Symbole. Entscheide, welches der unten angegebenen Wörter in die jeweilige Lücke passt.

Gregory: My problem is that my grandfather lives with us. We're not allowed to leave things around on the floor, because he sometimes falls down. He leaves his ____________ ◆ teeth in the bathroom – really yucky! But the worst thing is that he doesn't listen to other people's ______________ ◇, not ________ ▼ my parents', and especially not mine, because I'm "only" twelve. He chooses the TV_______________________ ◇ we watch. He thinks he's more ____________________ ▼ than anybody ____________ ◆. I wish he would move out.

Words to practise:
◆ false – else; ◇ opinions – programmes; ▼ important – even

Tom: Our parents want us to be babies for _______________ ◆. My uncle bought me a ___________ ◇-board for ________________ △, but I'm not allowed to use it, because it's "too dangerous". I've got a _______________ ◆, but that doesn't make any difference. They even get ______________ △ if I go out on my bike. And my sister isn't allowed to wear _____________ ▼. I mean, she's fourteen! We're not allowed to go to the local _____________ ◇ club; we could meet the "wrong" people. They just don't want us to _________ ▼ up.

Words to practise:
◆ ever – helmet; ◇ skate – youth; △ Christmas – nervous;
▼ jewellery – grow

Rebecca: My parents don't give me ___________ ◆ pocket money. I only buy normal things, like magazines, snacks, cinema tickets, cassettes ________ ▼, but by the middle of the month I've spent every penny. I think my mum and dad are ______________ ◆ out of touch with the real world. If I ask for more money they give me a very ___________ ◇ answer: "No, you can't". Any sort of ____________ ◇ is out of the question. I could get a Saturday job, but that's not the point. I should be ________ ▼ to spend money on things I want, without having a job.

Words to practise:
◆ enough – completely; ◇ dialogue – short; ▼ etc. – able

2. **Hier ist der Anfang der Antwort auf einen der Briefe. Von wem ist der Brief?**

Try keeping a record of the money you spend; how much, and what for. Show it to your parents at the end of the month.

Gregory / Tom / Rebecca

3. a) Im Text kommt eine gängige Abkürzung vor. Welche? ________

b) Unterstreiche die entsprechende deutsche Abkürzung:
bzw. – usw. – u. Ä.

4. **Schreibe die Lernwörter der drei Texte hin, die die Laute [f] (2-mal) und [v] (3-mal) haben.**

[f] __________ __________

[v] __________ __________ __________

5. **Schreibe die Lernwörter hin, die den Laut [s] enthalten.**

[s] __________ __________ __________

__________ __________ __________

6. Die fast-Homophone *falls – false*

a) Welches Wort gehört zu dem jeweiligen Zeichen? Schreibe es hin.

If you put a stone into water it □ straight to the bottom. Is this statement true or ●?

□ ____________ ● ____________

b) Setze die passenden Wörter ein.

There's a climber on the North Face of the Eiger. He's a good climber, and he never _________. That's good, because he hasn't got a rope. If he makes a ___________ move, he may die.

7. Die fast-Homophone *bought – board*

a) Entschlüssele die Symbole:

Daniel's dad got a lot of presents for his fiftieth birthday. His wife ▼ him a new watch and Daniel made a chess ▽ for him.

▼ _____________ ▽ _____________

b) Setze die Wörter jetzt selber ein.

Form 9a collects money for 'fun' things. So far they've _____________ some playing cards and some _____________ games for break-times on rainy days.

8. Dies ist eine Forderung, nach der im 19. Jahrhundert viele Kinder erzogen wurden. Finde sie in der Buchstabenschlange. Aber Achtung: Nur jedes zweite Wort gehört zu dem Satz.

OPINIONCHILDRENELSESHOULDNERVOUSBEENOUGHSEENEVERANDCHRISTMASNOTYOUTHHEARD!

Fange mit dem zweiten Wort an. **Tipp**

An interview with a young actor

In der neuesten Ausgabe von *Scrapbook* findet man ein Interview mit einem jungen Schauspieler.

9. **Ergänze den Text mit den folgenden Wörtern. Der erste Buchstabe ist jeweils angegeben.**

actor *actress* *article* *autumn* *cameras* *character* *copied* *Christmas* *combination* *dad* *drama* *factory* *following* *happened* *heroes* *improve* *interview* *organize* *other* *plans* *photo* *stop* *studied*

Scrapbook: When did you first start acting, Steve?

Steve: Well, we had d__________ lessons at school. At the end of the a__________ term there was a Christmas show with sketches about the teachers. I was the Maths teacher. I c__________ the way he walked, and everybody just fell about laughing.

Scrapbook: When did you decide to become an a__________?

Steve: I think it was at the end of that C__________ show. The sight and sound of all those people clapping and shouting was fantastic.

Scrapbook: Are there any o__________ actors in your family?

Steve: Yes, on my mother's side of the family. My mother wanted to be an a____________, too, but her father didn't allow it. Acting is her hobby now. My d______'s in the film business, but he works behind the scenes, not in front of the c______________.

Scrapbook: So you're f________________ in their footsteps. What h____________________ after the Christmas show?

Steve: Well, then I acted in the school play, and later I started to o______________ it. I usually played the main c________________. Sometimes there was an a__________ in the local newspaper, with a p____________. Then we felt like h__________.

Scrapbook: Did you have enough time for your school work?

Steve: My parents always said I must s__________ acting and concentrate on school work. But I couldn't stop acting. Anyway, I managed to get three A-levels. It was a funny c____________________: English, French and Biology.

Scrapbook: What did you do after you left school?

Steve: I wanted to i______________ my French, so I got a job in a f_____________ in France. It was boring, but I learned a lot of French. Then I s__________________ drama in London.

Scrapbook: Have you got any p__________ for the future?

Steve: I'd like to work in America.

Scrapbook: Well good luck, Steve! And thank you very much for the i________________.

10. **Einige der Lernwörter sind so genannte *false friends*, das heißt, sie sind im Deutschen und Englischen sehr ähnlich, aber doch nicht ganz gleich. Ergänze.**

a) There was an __rti_____ and a __oto in the newspaper about the school play.

b) One of the __haracters in the play was a thief.

c) Steve enjoyed __rama lessons at school.

d) The journalist from Scrapbook thanked Steve for the __nterview.

e) Steve has got a __lan for the future.

f) He can't sto__ acting.

g) He can __opy the way people walk.

Tipp

Achte besonders auf die Groß- und Kleinschreibung.

11. Zwei Wörter in der Liste haben einen stummen Konsonanten – einmal ein „n" und einmal ein „t".

________________ ________________

12. Hier sind unbetonte Vokale ausgelassen worden. Ergänze sie.

act__r aut__mn fact__r__ org__n__ze

13. Bei Wörtern, die mit „o" enden, wird der Plural unterschiedlich gebildet. Ergänze die Reihe:

Singular	Plural
hero	________________
________________	photos

14. Die ähnlich klingenden Wörter *side – sight*

a) Ergänze die passenden Wörter bei den Symbolen:

We wanted to see the ❁s of London, so we went on a ❁-seeing tour. We sat on the right-hand ⌘ of the bus.

⌘ ________________ ❁ ________________

b) Versuche es jetzt ohne die Hilfe von Symbolen.

It was very strange to see the traffic on the left-hand _______ of the road. Crossing from one __________ of the road to the other can be dangerous. It's best to wait until there is no traffic in __________.

15. Revision: Die Homophone *your – you're*

a) Entschlüssele:

If ◇ going to buy a new bike, you should sell ◆ old one.

◆ ________________   ◇ ________________

b) Setze ein:

Just imagine: ____________ saving money to buy a new bike, because ____________ old one is too small for you. But __________ lucky; you win a bike in a competition. What do you do with all ________ money?

16. Das kürzeste Theaterstück der Welt wurde von Samuel Beckett geschrieben und heißt *Breath.* Wie lange dauert es? Neben der richtigen Schreibweise steht die Antwort auf die Frage.

actres	half an hour
Chrismas	twenty minutes
autumn	thirty seconds
caracter	a quarter of an hour

Homeless children in Mexico

17. **Ergänze den Text mit den angegebenen Wörtern. Neben jeder Lücke steht die deutsche Übersetzung in der jeweiligen Grundform.**

activities *design* *empty* *Europe* *Europeans* *factory*
grew up *heads* *hours* *pavement* *reach* *receive* *rescued*
scary *sell* *sell* *smuggling* *sold* *study* *washes*

Diese Woche kann man in *Scrapbook* erfahren, wie es den Straßenkindern in Mexiko geht.

For ______________ **(Europäer)**, it's hard to imagine what life is like on the streets of Mexico. A lot of parents don't make enough money to buy clothes and food for their families, so their children have to work, too. Some sell sweets, others wash cars or clean people's shoes for them on the ________________ **(Gehweg)**. Life on the streets isn't much fun! Today there is an organization called MAMA, and its job is to help these children. Teachers from MAMA go into the streets to try to ______________ **(erreichen)** these children.

Manuel is twelve years old and has no parents. He ________________ **(aufwachsen)** on the streets and __________ **(verkaufen)** chewing gum until MAMA _____________ **(retten)** him. Now he lives in a home for boys. He has made a lot of friends there, and enjoys football and other ______________ **(Aktivitäten)**.

Catarino, sixteen, left home because he thought life on the streets must be better. But he found that it was ____________ **(unheimlich)**, especially at night. He slept in an ____________ **(leer)** box. There were people around him fighting and _______________ **(schmuggeln)** drugs. Now he is able to sleep at MAMA's night shelter, where he can also wash, eat, and play table-football with his mates. He _____________ **(waschen)** cars in the day time, but he would like to work in a _____________ **(Fabrik)** one day.

Rosa lives at home. She's fourteen, and she goes to school for two _____________ **(Stunde)** each day. Then she goes out with her sister to

_____________ **(verkaufen)** sweets. One day she would like to _______________ **(studieren)** architecture and ____________ **(entwerfen)** buildings, or perhaps teach in a school.

Unlike kids in ___________ **(Europa)**, the children of the streets in Mexico are very poor, and they're lucky if they _______________ **(erhalten)** any schooling, or even have enough food and a roof over their _____________ **(Kopf)**. The director of MAMA hopes that his organization will improve life in Mexico.

18. **Finde drei Wörter in der Auswahl zu Übung 17 mit dem Laut [j] (wie in *you*). Schreibe sie auf.**

__________________ __________________ ________________

19. **Welche zwei Wörter in der Auswahl zu Übung 17 haben einen stummen Konsonanten?**

_________________ _______________

20. **Ergänze die Wörter mit folgenden Buchstabenpaaren: *ea – ie – ei*.**

r___ch bel__ve l__ve rec__ve activit__s

Welches Wort unterscheidet sich von den anderen? ______________

21. **Schreibe die Grundform der folgenden Wörter hin.**

a) sold _____________ b) smuggling _____________

c) activities _____________ d) washes _____________

e) rescued _____________ f) grew up _____________

22. Die ähnlich klindenden Wörter *made – mate*

a) Entschlüssele:

Catarino has ◆ a lot of friends at the night shelter. He says "I often play table-football with my ◇ Mario".

◆ ______________________ ◇ ______________________

b) Setze ein:

Rosa is helping a class_______ to write a story. Her class______ has ______ some mistakes.

23. Did you know ...?

In Mexico, a lot of people live in a small space. It is the most ...

a◯tivity Eu◯ope h◯urs gro◯

sol◯ pav◯ment ◯esign

... city in the world.

A trip to France

Der Schulchor der *Backwell High School* reiste im Rahmen eines musikalischen Austausches nach Frankreich. Holly schrieb ein Tagebuch und schickte es hinterher an die Redaktion von *Scrapbook*. Sie fand es interessant und druckte es.

24. Ergänze den Text mit folgenden Wörtern.

above bacon boat cassette choir combined concert conversation dictionary exchange journeys map popular religious slow souvenirs suitcase toilets travel whistling

Tipp Die Konsonanten sind angegeben, die Vokale musst du ergänzen.

Sunday: Packed my ______________ **(stcs)**, including a present for the family I'm staying with and (very important!) a

French ____________________ **(dctnry)**. Found Arles on a _________ **(mp)** of Europe.

Monday: I don't like train ______________ **(jrnys)**! Why didn't we ____________ **(trvl)** by plane? It's too hot on this train and the _______________ **(tlts)** are smelly. The ___________ **(bt)** over to France was much more fun, with the sky ___________ **(bv)** us and the sea all around.

Tuesday: Arrived here last night. The family is friendly, but ______________________ **(cnvrstn)** is ___________ **(slw)** and we use the dictionary a lot. Marie's mum cooked ____________ **(bcn)** and eggs for breakfast this morning. Actually, I would like to eat French food while I'm here. That's the idea of an _______________ **(xchng)**. Anyway, I always have cornflakes at home.

Wednesday: Choir practice today, just for our ___________ **(chr)**. In the concert the French choir is going to sing first, then us, then both together for the last piece.

Thursday: Practised the last piece with ________________ **(cmbnd)** choirs this morning. The French choir is quite good. Trip to the seaside in the afternoon – half an hour on the bus. Bought some _______________ **(svnrs)**, including a mouse made out of a stone, for Mum's collection. Must buy something for Dad, too.

Friday: Am writing this in bed. Have had a fantastic day. Trip to Arles in the morning, practised in the afternoon and __________________ **(cncrt)** in the evening. The French choir sang a ____________________ **(rlgs)** piece and some ____________________ **(pplr)** songs. At first I was really nervous and my mouth felt dry. One of the French teachers recorded the concert on __________________ **(csstt)**. Not sure if I want to hear it!

Saturday: On the train again. Toilets still smelly and journey boring, but everybody is ____________________ **(whstlng)** and singing French songs and talking about the exchange. I wonder if the French kids will like England.

25. Schreibe die Betonungsmuster für diese Wörter.

a) popular _____ b) religious _______

c) souvenirs _______ d) conversation ______

Tipp

Erinnerst du dich noch? Für eine betonte Silbe nimmst du **O,** für eine unbetonte **o**. Für *popular* würde dann das Betonungsmuster lauten: Ooo.

26. Unterstreiche die Vokale in den folgenden Wörtern, die mit dem Laut [ə] ausgesprochen werden (für jedes Wort einer).

cassette *bacon* *combined* *concert* *popular* *souvenirs*

27. Ein Wort aus der Auswahl hat zwei stumme Konsonanten. Schreibe die Grundform davon hin.

____

28. Finde zwei Wörter mit dem Laut [ʃ], wie in *shake* oder *dish*:

___________ ________________

und zwei mit dem Laut [dʒ], wie in *jump* oder *bridge*:

_____________ ______________

29. Füge die fehlenden Buchstaben ein.

Su◯tcase relig◯ous dict◯onary

popul◯r cho◯r journ◯y

30. Die ähnlich klingenden Wörter *mouth – mouse*

a) Entschlüssele:

You put food in your ✳ when you eat. A ✻ is only small, so it only puts a little bit of food in its ✳.

✻ ______________ ✳ ______________

b) Füge die Wörter ein:

If you see a _________ , what do you do? Open your _________ and scream?

31. Revision: die Homophone *here – hear*

a) Entschlüssele:

▶ is the doorbell. If I don't ◁ it, just knock on this window ▶, okay?

▶ ______________ ◁ ______________

b) Setze ein:

If you sit at the back of the class, you won't be able to _______ very well. Sit ________, near the blackboard.

32. In welchem Teil Frankreiches waren Holly und ihre Mitmusiker? Verbinde die Wörter links mit den richtigen Definitionen rechts. Die Buchstaben neben der passenden Definition ergeben das Lösungswort.

choir	opposite of quick	U
dictionary	exchange of ideas in the form of speech	T
slow	a group of people who sing together	S
conversation	opposite of below	H
above	a book where you can look up words	O

Holly and her friends were in the ______________ of France.

Favourite sports

Scrapbook bringt diese Woche einen Artikel über die Lieblingssportarten der LeserInnen. Mandy liest gern alles über Sport.

33. **Ergänze den Text mit folgenden Wörtern.**

calendar *cricket* *cycling* *engine* *exercise* *flight* *grown* *healthy* *hockey* *horse* *jacket* *life* *metre* *motor* *national* *noisy* *opinion* *proof* *queue* *reach* *received* *sailing* *skiing* *slow* *special* *straight* *suitable* *tall* *unit*

We [rɪ'si:vd] ________________ hundreds of letters about your favourite sports. We couldn't print them all – sorry!

Susan: I love riding. It's a very ['helθɪ] ______________ sport, and anybody can do it. You need ['su:təbl] ________________ clothing, like riding boots and a hard hat. A riding ['dʒækɪt] _______________ is useful, too. I have my own [hɔ:s] ______________, called Captain. Once he threw me off, but I got [streɪt] _____________ back on.

Jamie: I play ['krɪkɪt] _____________. It's quite a [sləʊ] ___________ game, and I know that some people find it boring, but I like it. I've [grəʊn] ___________ up with cricket; my father plays, too. In summer my ['kælɪndə] ___________ is full of matches. In winter I play football and ['hɒki] _________.

Daniel: My sister and I belong to a ['seɪlɪŋ] ______________ club. Some of the boats have a ['məʊtə] __________, but it's just for emergencies. It's like ['saɪklɪŋ] _____________ or walking: you travel without an ['endʒɪn] _______________. There's no danger if you follow the rules and wear a [laɪf] _______-jacket.

Annemarie: I often go to the local dry ski slope. Last winter I went ['ski:ɪŋ] ____________ in Switzerland on real snow – fantastic! Even the [kju:] ____________ for the ski-lift was fun – I met lots of nice boys! It was my first [flaɪt] ____________ in a plane, too. I loved taking off and flying through the air.

Lee: Some people have the idea that only [tɔ:l] ____________ people play basketball, so that they can [ri:tʃ] ____________ the net. I'm only one ['mi:tə] ____________ sixty-six, and I think I'm living [pru:f] __________ that they're wrong. I play in the school team. Each person has his own ['speʃl] _____________ job within the team, but we work together as a ['ju:nɪt] _____________.

Trefor: I'm from Wales, and rugby is our ['næʃnəl] _______________ sport. The popular [ə'pɪnjən] ______________ is that rugby players are ['nɔɪzi] ______________, and drink too much beer. Well, perhaps we do shout. So what? And you need to drink a lot after all that ['eksəsaɪz] ________________!

34. a) Wie viele Schreibweisen für den Vokal [i:] findest du in der Auswahl? Schreibe die Wörter hin:

____

Tipp Insgesamt kannst du vier Wörter finden.

b) Du kennst andere Schreibweisen für [i:]. Ergänze die Sätze:

You n___d a k___ to open a door.

Have a p___ce of cake.

35. In der Liste gibt es drei Wörter, die mit unbetontem [ə] enden.

a) Schreib sie hier hin:

__________ __________ __________

b) In den Texten bei Jamie und bei Lee findest du diesen Laut in wieder anderen Schreibweisen.

__________ __________

36. Finde Wörter in der Liste, die sich mit diesen hier reimen.

a) phone __________ b) white __________

c) (of) course __________ d) wait __________ e) so __________

37. In drei Wörtern findest du den Laut [u:]. Schreibe sie hier hin.

____

38. a) Welche drei Lernwörter haben den Laut [ʃ], wie in *shoe* oder *wash*?

__________ __________

b) Finde ein Wort im Beitrag von Trefor mit noch einer anderen Schreibweise für diesen Laut.

____

39. Die Homophone *two* – *too*

a) Entschlüssele:

We're going to spend ◆ or three hours on the beach.
Are you coming, ▲? – No, thanks, it's ▲ hot.

◆ ____________________ ▲ ____________________

b) Füge die Wörter ein:

Some pizzas are big enough for ______ people. They're ______ big for one person. So share a pizza with a friend. It's fun, and it's cheaper, ______!

40. Im Sommer betreibt Jamie eine Sportart, die er nicht verraten will. Er hat sie seinen Freunden aber verschlüsselt hingeschrieben.

Jamie also plays ✻◆▼▲ ___________.

Vervollständige die Wörter, dann hast du fast schon Jamies Lieblingssportart.

pr◆◆▲ en✻ine ◆pini◆n hea▼thy

What the girls think of Prince William

Scrapbook bat Leserinnen, ihre Meinung über Prince William der Zeitschrift zu schreiben.

41. Ergänze den Text mit folgenden Wörtern:

able *activities* *articles* *bathroom* *born* *detectives* *disco*
divorced *even* *example* *famous* *free* *imagine* *including*
king *kisses* *knock* *people* *popular* *Queen* *quite* *silly*
situation *special* *suitable* *thought* *type*

Scrapbook asked readers what they t___________ of the future king of England. Some of you felt sorry for him …

Laura, 14, of Lincoln: His parents got d_____________ when he was q_______ young. That's bad enough; but every day there were a_______________ in the newspapers about it. How could anybody live with a s_______________ like that?

Harriet, 14, of Wokingham: If William goes to a d_________, k_______ a girl or just goes down to the shops, the newspapers are watching him. And it's no good putting on sun glasses and a big hat. They know who he is!

Kelly, 14, of Durley: His mum died when he was only 15. The whole world was shocked – i__________________ what it was like for her sons, William and Harry.

Hannah, 14, of Tamworth: He's Prince Charles's son, and he will have to be k______ one day. He's not f_____ to choose his own life – he has to do what the Q________ says. She e________ checks his girlfriends to see if they're s_______________.

Helen, 17, of Witney: D_____________ watch his a____________ 24 hours a day. Of course, these men are there to look after him – but it can't be much fun for him. He can never just go out and do something s_________.

Other readers didn't feel so sorry for him …

Adrienne, 16, of Watford: This boy has had a horse, a car and a servant as birthday presents, and at school he had his own private b______________. I bet he has never repaired a hole in his jeans or done a newspaper round! He'll never have to k______ on doors asking for a job.

Emily, 15, of Harrow: Most famous p____________ have done something s___________. William is f____________ just because he was b_______ into the right family.

Diane, 14, of Richmond: He should set a good e____________ to young people, but he doesn't. He goes hunting for foxes. I'm not sorry for somebody who thinks it's right to kill animals!

Ruth, 17, of Deal: William is lucky. He's got blond hair and blue eyes, and he's a really good looking, friendly t________ of person, so of course he's p__________ with women, i__________ famous ones like Britney Spears and Princess Caroline of Monaco.

42. Zeichne Betonungsmuster (O = betonte Silbe, o = unbetonte Silbe) für folgende Wörter:

imagine oOo activities ______ popular ______ famous ______
including ______ detectives ______ divorced ______ situation ______
special ______ suitable ______ articles ______

43. Welches Wort wird [nɒk] ausgesprochen? __________

44. Schreibe den Infinitiv (Grundform) oder den Singular zu folgenden Wörtern hin:

articles ______ kisses ______ putting ______
detectives ______ activities ______ repaired ______
including ______

45. Revision: die Homophone *whole* – *hole*

a) Entschlüssele:
A pet rabbit usually spends its ✻ life in a cage, but a wild rabbit lives in a ◆ in a hillside.

◆ __________ ✻ __________

b) Setze ein:

If you get a ________ in your bicycle tyre, you can repair it, or you can buy a ________ new tyre.

46. Revision: die Homophone *sun* – *son*

a) Entschlüssele:
The ▽ was shining, so Rachel took her three daughters and her △ to the seaside.

△ __________ ▽ __________

b) Setze ein:

Richard is taking his ________, Alan, camping at the weekend. They plan to get up when the ________ comes up, and go to bed when the ________ goes down.

47. In welcher Funktion spielte Prinz William in den Mannschaften? Ergänze den Satz unten. Die fehlenden Buchstaben ergeben die Lösung.

situa_ion	que_n	f_mous	i_agine	spe_ial	
suit_ble	cu_board	de_ective	popul_r	d_vorced	ki_g.

Tipp

Nimm die bestehende Reihenfolge der Buchstaben.

Prince William loves sport. At Ludgrove School, where he went from the age of 8 to 13, he was rugby and hockey

— — — —   — — — — — — — .

Debbie's worst day

Scrapbook veröffentlicht in jeder Ausgabe Berichte über besondere Erlebnisse einzelner LeserInnen. In dieser Woche ist es Debbie.

48. Ergänze den Text mit den fehlenden Wörtern. Die Zeichen helfen dir.

○ candle, disabled	❁ office, packet	⌘ technology, festival
▷ entrance, statue	∗ telephone, labels	◆ slogan, ambulance
▽ corridor, pilot	□ weather, special	➽ head, frightened
✂ ridden, trousers	▲ authentic, sign	

Facts about Debbie:

Age: 13; star sign: Leo; favourite food: bacon sandwiches; favourite colour: blue; loves: horses, _______________ ○ light; hates: cigarette smoke.

One day in the Easter holidays, my mum and I made up a _________________ ❁ of sandwiches and went to meet Aunt Margaret, my mum's sister, at the stables *(Reitstall)* to practise for a riding __________________ ⌘. The _________________ □ was terrible – the wind was coming off the sea, and it blew rain into our faces.

My aunt rode off first. When Mum got on her horse, her new waterproof ___________________ ✗ made a loud rustling *(zischen)* sound. The horse was _________________ ➽ and galloped straight past my aunt, over the road and up a farm track.

Mum fell off, and when I saw her, I knew that it was serious. We didn't have a mobile phone with us, so my aunt ran back to the stables to use the ___________________ ∗, while I held Mum's hand. Soon an ____________________ ◆ arrived, but the paramedics said she needed an air ambulance. Driving over the bumpy track might make her _________________ ○ for life.

Ten long minutes passed before the helicopter landed. It was just like a film, but this was ________________ ▲, the real thing. The paramedics loaded Mum onto a ________________ □ board and put her into the back of the helicopter, ________________ ➧ first, so that she could see the ________________ ▽. I wasn't allowed to go with her, so my aunt drove me to the hospital. At the ________________ ▷ there was a sign with the ______________ ◆: "While there's life, there's hope". My aunt had to ________________ ▲ a form in an ______________ ❁, then we went down a long ________________ ▽ and found Mum with a big machine next to the bed. There were tubes and bottles with strange ________________ ∗ around her. She needed modern ________________ ⌘ to help her to live.

Now, seven months later, she is nearly back to normal. Dusty stands as still as a ________________ ▷ when anyone gets on her, but Mum has never ____________ ✂ her again!

49. **Zeichne Betonungsmuster für diese Wörter:**

technology *oOoo* ______ packet _____ pilot _____

frightened _____ special ______

50. **Drei der Lernwörter haben den (betonten) Vokal [aɪ], wie in *why*, *right*, *fine*. Welche sind es?**

____________ ____________ ____________

51. **Welches der drei Wörter aus Übung 48 reimt sich auf *mine*?**

____

Unterstreiche den stummen Konsonanten in diesem Wort.

Du kennst noch ein Wort, das ganz ähnlich ist: d _ s _ _ _

52. Erkennst du diese Wörter aus der Auswahl von Übung 48? Sie stehen in der Lautschrift und haben alle etwas von der Aussprache her gemeinsam. Was wohl?

['festɪvl] ______________ ['leɪbl] ______________

['kændl] ______________

Sie enden alle mit dem Laut [___]

Schau die Wörter in der normalen Schreibweise an. Was fällt dir hinsichtlich der Rechtschreibung auf?

Es gibt hier __________ (wie viele?) verschiedene Schreibweisen für denselben Endlaut.

53. Die Homophone *past* – *passed*

a) Unterstreiche *past* / *passed* mit verschiedenen Farben. Zeichne dann einen Kreis um jedes Verb (in einem Fall besteht das Verb aus *have* + *past participle*) in jedem Satz. Was kannst du über den Unterschied zwischen *past* und *passed* sagen?

The bus left at half past three. It passed the church at quarter to four. At five past four the bus suddenly stopped. Three minutes passed. Then the driver drove slowly past some traffic lights. We passed some archaeologists. In the past, this place was a Roman theatre. Lots of people have passed this place. Not many of them know about its past.

b) Entschlüssele:
Dad, we've just ▼ the new ice cream café. Don't just drive ✻! It's only quarter ✻ two. Let's call in.

✻ ______________ ▼ ______________

c) Setze ein:

In the ________, Dad always bought us ice creams. He couldn't drive ________ a café without stopping. But today we've _________ three or four nice cafés. We ate at half __________ twelve, and it's already ten __________ three. When we __________ the last café, we shouted "Please stop, Dad!" But he went straight ___________. He's on a diet, you see.

54. Revision: die Homophone *rode* – *road*

a) Entschlüssele:
Yesterday Fabian and Paul ◇ their bikes along the main ◆ to the next town.

◆ ______________ ◇ ______________

b) Setze ein:

Last Saturday, Jane, Mandy and Daniel went to the old castle. Jane and Daniel _________ their bikes, and Mandy ________ her horse. Jane and Daniel cycled along the __________, but Mandy said the _________ was too dangerous for her horse, so she took a field path.

55. Die Homophone *a loud* – *allowed*

a) Entschlüssele:
"You're not △ to run in the corridors," said Mr Norton in ▶ voice.

△ ______________ ▶ ______________

b) Setze ein:

Do you know the game "murder in the dark"? You need about eight people. There are two "detectives" who aren't _____________ to come into the dark room until they hear ______________ scream. Then there's ___________ knock on the door, and the detectives come in. They're _______________ to question everybody until they find the "murderer".

56. Das ungleiche Zwillingspaar *life* – *live*

a) Diese zwei Wörter sind keine Homophone; sie werden völlig unterschiedlich ausgesprochen. Finde von jedem Wort ein Beispiel im Text von Übung 48. Markiere es und schreibe es dann zusammen mit dem vorhergehenden Wort in die richtige Schreibzeile.

[laɪf] ______________________ [lɪv] ______________________

b) In dem Satz steckt ein wichtiger Unterschied zwischen beiden Wörtern. Ergänze ihn.

__________ ist ein Verb und ___________ ist ein Nomen.

c) Entschlüssele:
A hamster's □ is quite short. Hamsters only ■ for about two years.

■ _______________ □ ________________

d) Setze ein:

When he was a young man, Thor Heyerdahl wanted to escape from modern ________, so he and his wife went to _________ on an island in the Pacific Ocean. They found that _________ wasn't easy. They didn't ________ near the sea with the island people. They wanted to _________ in the jungle. After a few months they went to _______ on another island where there was a doctor. Thor's wife was ill, and the doctor saved her ________.

57. **Auch Pferde haben ihre eigene „Sprache", durch die wir zum Teil herausfinden können, wie es ihnen geht. Was macht zum Beispiel ein Pferd, wenn es wütend ist? Jedes zweite Wort in der Kette gibt Auskunft. Die Botschaft fängt mit dem Zweiten Wort an und endet mit dem letzten Wort.**

CANDLEANENTRANCEANGRYPILOTHORSEAMBULANCEPUTSTELEPHONEITSHEADEARSSTATUEBACK

C Word workshop 1

1. Pluralformen

> Den Plural bildest du, indem du ein **-s** anhängst. Bei Wörtern, die auf einen Zischlaut enden (zum Beispiel *match*, *crash*, *class*), hängst du ein **-es** an, weil du das Wort sonst nicht aussprechen könntest.

1. Schreibe neben die folgenden Pluralformen hin, wie viele Silben die Wörter haben.

a) cheeses ____ b) bridges ____ c) brushes ____

d) horses ____ e) addresses ___ f) crisps ___

g) ages ___ h) baths ___ i) services ___

j) ambulances ___ k) languages ___ l) clothes ___

Tipp

Wenn -*es* angehängt wird, dann ergibt es (meist) eine Silbe mehr.

2. Bilde den Plural.

a) waitress___ b) accident___ c) prize___

d) garage___ e) ghost___ f) dish___

g) key___ h) size___ i) concert___

j) entrance___ k) forest___ l) match___

m) wish___ n) bus___ o) church___

3. Hier haben wir es mit einem Sonderfall zu tun. Gib die Grundform an.

a) emergencies____________________ b) bodies____________________

c) diaries____________________

4. **Bilde die Pluralform.**

a) factory ______________ b) assembly ______________

c) ferry ____________ d) dictionary ______________

e) activity _____________ f) hobby ____________

5. **Einige Wörter enden mit Vokal + y. Gib den Singular an.**

a) boys ___________ b) holidays __________________

Bilde hier die Pluralform:

c) way___________ d) journey_____________ e) toy_____________

6. **Einige englische und deutsche Wörter sind sich sehr ähnlich, darum kann man sie leicht verwechseln. Schreibe den Plural zu diesen Wörtern hin.**

a) kindergarten ______________________

b) rucksack ______________________

c) hobby ______________________

Tipp

Du erinnerst dich vielleicht: Besonders in der Groß- und Kleinschreibung, aber auch bei der Pluralbildung unterscheiden sich Englisch und Deutsch, zum Beispiel: Englisch: *kindergarten – kindergartens*; Deutsch: Kindergarten – Kindergärten.

7. **Es gibt noch einige andere ähnliche Wörter. Ergänze die Singular- oder Pluralform.**

Singular	Plural
a) bank	*banks*
b) ______________	detectives
c) concert	______________
d) ________________	programmes
e) situation	________________

f) ______________ cassettes

g) character ______________

h) ______________ articles

i) tourist ______________

j) ______________ statues

k) farmer ______________

l) ______________ dialogues

m) ______________ taxis

8. Ein bestimmter Buchstabe fehlt hier. Welcher ist es?

p-tat- *t-mat-* *radi-* *her-* *kil-* *s-l-* *disc-* *ph-t-*

a) Der Buchstabe ______ fehlt.

b) Drei der Wörter oben bilden den **Plural mit -es**, die anderen nur mit **-s**. Welche drei sind es? Schreibe gleich die Pluralform hin.

______________ ______________ ______________

9. Ergänze die Sätze. Die Wörter findest du in Klammern im Singular.

a) Most ______________ have at least two ______________ in the house. **(radio, family)**

b) Most ______________ are in ______________. **(city, factory)**

c) The ______________ have got new ______________. Our postman has two interesting ______________: collecting stamps and keeping ______________. **(budgie, postman, hobby, uniform)**

d) Toby's mum and dad made many ______________ to foreign ______________ when they were younger. **(journey, country)**

e) They took ______________ of ______________ and of old buildings, especially ______________. **(photo, church, statue)**

f) When they went to Switzerland they took French, Italian and German ____________________ with them in their ____________________, together with the ______________ of some friends they had in Zurich. **(address, dictionary, rucksack)**

g) They didn't have much money, so they ate mostly ________________, cheese and nice red ________________. **(tomato, potato)**

h) One day they were able to rescue two children from a river. The children's parents said they were ______________, and gave them tickets for two ________________ and some tennis ________________. **(match, concert, hero)**

10. **Ergänze.**

half	______________
______________	shelves
wife	______________
______________	lives [laɪvz]

2. Die 3. Person Singular

11. **Ergänze den Text mit diesen Wörtern:**

washes *buys* *comes* *works* *tries* *does* *goes* *goes* *worries*

Toby's mother ____________ very hard in an office every day. Toby's father usually ____________ the clothes. He ____________ to work, too, but he ____________ a lot of his work at home. He always ____________ to be there when Toby ____________ home from school. He ______________ if

Toby is late. He ____________ shopping and ____________ most of the food for the family.

12. Ergänze die linke Spalte mit dem Infinitiv (Grundform) und die rechte mit der 3. Person Singular.

a) washes	______________	a) work	______________
b) worries	______________	b) go	______________
c) does	______________	c) come	______________
d) tries	______________	d) rescue	______________
e) copies	______________	e) finish	______________
f) improves	______________	f) buy	______________
g) receives	______________	g) kiss	______________
h) grows	______________	h) study	______________

13. Ergänze den Text mithilfe der Lautschrift.

Every day Fabian's dad [kʌmz] ______________ home from work, [kɪsɪz] ____________ his wife and [sez] ___________ hello to the children. His wife sometimes [gəʊz] _________ out and ['stʌdiz] ___________ French in the evening, so he ['fɪnɪʃɪz] ______________ the housework while Jasmin ['kɒpiz] _____________ pictures in her colouring book. Sometimes Fabian ['wɒʃɪz] _____________ the dishes, and Paul [traɪz] _________ to help, too.

3. -ing-Formen

14. Bei der Verlaufsform finden wir *-ing* am Ende des Verbs. Manchmal hängst du einfach *-ing* an, doch manchmal ändert sich auch etwas bei der Schreibung des Verbs. Unterstreiche die Verben, bei denen dies der Fall ist.

build come add go enjoy get disappear worry
change stop drive need drink overtake land forget
fly dance explain put

Bei neun dieser Verben nimmt man eine Änderung vor. **Tipp**

15. Gib jeweils den Infinitiv an:

a) making ____________ b) dropping ____________
c) cycling ____________ d) writing ____________
e) pulling ____________

16. Verwandle die *simple tenses* in *progressives.*

Beispiele: Sue often **makes** cakes. She**'s making** a cake now. **(present tense)**
David **made** a lot of model boats. He **was making** one when the storm started. **(past)**

a) Daniel and Andy always have a nice time at their grandmother's house. They ________________ a nice time there at the moment.

b) Toby's dad drives to work every weekday. He___ just ____________ the car out of the garage.

c) Paul ate three little cakes. He ______ just ____________ the last one when Maria spoke to him.

d) Mandy's mum speaks three languages. Just now she ________________ French on the phone.

e) Jane's little brother Alfie tried to carry a big box. He ________________ very hard, but he couldn't do it.

f) Jane and her mum carried the box for Alfie. They ______________________ it up the stairs when the phone rang.

g) Look, the car in front of us ______________________. You'll have to stop too, Dad!

h) I like writing stories. At the moment I ______________________ one about a monster.

17. Ergänze die Spalten.

Grundform	-ing-Form
a) copy	*copying*
b) ______________	organizing
c) agree	______________
d) ______________	travelling
e) smuggle	______________
f) ______________	skiing
g) cut	______________
h) ______________	clapping
i) sail	______________
j) ______________	kissing
k) knock	______________
l) ______________	selling
m) rescue	______________
n) ______________	whistling
o) include	______________
p) ______________	preparing
q) repeat	______________
r) ______________	combining

Die Ziffern geben die Position eines Buchstaben an. In der angegebenen Reihenfolge enthalten sie eine Botschaft.

n2 – p5 – d4 – l2 ______________ h3 _____

r4 – b2 – q4 – c1 – j1 ______________!

4. Das *simple past*

18. Schreibe den Infinitiv (Grundform) hin.

a) dropped ____________ b) carried ______________

c) watched ____________ d) decided ______________

19. Wie viele Silben haben diese Wörter? Schreibe die Anzahl hin.

a) decided _3_ b) agreed _2_ c) dropped _____

d) disappeared ____ e) married _____ f) jumped ____

g) saved _____ h) counted ____ i) checked _____

j) landed _____ k) called _____ l) guided _____

20. Schreibe das *simple past* dieser Verben hin.

a) exchange ________________ b) include ________________

c) kick ________________ d) study ________________

e) travel ________________ f) visit ________________

g) clap ________________ h) copy ________________

i) design ________________ j) finish ________________

k) follow ________________ l) own ________________

Tipp

Die Ziffern geben die Zahl der Buchstaben an:
a + b = 17; c + d = 13; e + f = 16; g + h = 13; i + j = 16; k + l = 13

21. In diesen Sätzen findest du Wörter in der Lautschrift. Einige enden auf *-ed*, andere nicht.

a) Aunt Sophie is ['marɪd] ________________. Her ['hʌzbənd] ______________________ is [kɔ:ld] _____________ Dave.

b) Daniel [θɔ:t] ________________ he [hɜ:d] ______________________ a noise [aut'saɪd] ________________ the door.

c) Fabian and his [frend] ______________ once [faʊnd] _______________ a little [bɜ:d] _____________ and they [held] _____________ it in their hands.

d) Toby [sed] ____________ that Daniel could watch the [wɜ:ld] _____________ Cup on TV at his house. Daniel was [pli:zd] _____________. He [təʊld] ______________ his mum, and he [steɪd] _____________ at Toby's all afternoon. He ['wɒntɪd] ____________ to [spend] ____________ the night there, but he wasn't [ə'laʊd] ______________ to do that.

e) It's too [kəʊld] ___________ to [raɪd] _______________ a bike today. We've [dɪ'saɪdɪd] _________________ to go to the cinema by bus.

f) Last week we [wɒtʃt] _______________ "A ['hʌndrəd] ________________ and one dalmations". On the way home we [stɒpt] ________________ to buy a magazine.

g) Sarah is in a wheelchair, because she's [dɪs'eɪbld] _________________. She's learning the piano, and two weeks ago she [pleɪd] ________________ in a concert. She was nervous and a bit [fraɪtnd] ________________, but she did well and everybody [klæpt] ______________ when she ['fɪnɪʃt] ___________________ playing.

5. Adjektive und Adverbien

22. Unterstreiche die Adjektive und Adverbien in diesem Satz. Es sind insgesamt fünf.

The smallest cups are empty, but the bigger ones are nearly full.

Welche Adjektive erscheinen in dem Satz in der Grundform?

__________________ __________________

Welche Endungen kommen vor?

__________ _____________ _____________

23. Gib die Grundform an.

angrily ______________ carefully ______________

correctly ______________ bigger ______________

funnier ______________ noisiest ______________

nicest ______________

24. Ergänze die Sätze mit den passenden Adverbien. Der erste Buchstabe ist vorgegeben.

angry | *beautiful* | *busy* | *careful* | *cheap* | *healthy* | *kind*
~~nervous~~ | *noisy* | *quiet* | *religious* | *slow* | *stupid* | *sudden* | *usual*

a) Sarah waited n*ervously*___ for the beginning of the concert.

b) Bob is 81 years old. He's a vegetarian and he goes swimming twice a week. He lives very h______________.

c) Jane was late, but Iris k______________ waited for her.

d) Alfie u__________ lies in bed q____________, but this evening he's singing n___________.

e) Mrs Brown thinks she's too fat, so she's keeping r________________ to a strict diet.

f) Iris writes b__________________, but rather s________________. It takes her an hour to write a letter to her penfriend.

g) The whole family is decorating the living room. They're working b___________ but c___________________.

h) S________________ Dad says a________________: Oh no! I've dropped some paint on the floor, and, very s__________________, I've stepped in it.

i) You can often buy good stuff very c_________________ at jumble sales *(Flohmärkte)*.

25. **Steigerung der Adjektive.** Ergänze die Sätze mit dem angegebenen Adjektiv.

Tipp

Achte auf den Inhalt der Sätze, damit du die richtige Endung *-er* oder *-est* wählst.

a) Yesterday the temperature was 29 degrees, and today it's even __________ than that; 32 degrees! **(hot)**

b) Today is the __________ day of the year so far. **(hot)**

c) Iris thinks her grandma is the ___________ person she knows. **(kind)**

d) Jane took Alfie to the circus. He said that the _________________ part was the clown's act. **(funny)**

e) This morning was _________________ than this afternoon. **(sunny)**

f) Now it's raining. Daniel is playing football at the playground. He's getting ____________ and _____________. **(wet)**

g) Daniel's brother Andy has gone home, so he's much ______________ than Daniel. **(dry)**

26. Auch hier geht es um die Steigerung der Adjektive. Ergänze.

a) The ______________ person in Form 9a is Quentin, a new boy from Leeds. **(noisy)**

b) The weather again! Today it's __________________ than yesterday. It looks like rain. **(cloudy)**

c) Chocolate ice cream is _______________ than vanilla ice cream. Or don't you agree? **(nice)**

d) Robert's dad does a lot of sport and eats healthily. He's ___________ than his wife, but he's not the ___________ in the family. Robert is __________ than his dad. **(fit)**

e) Have you heard the ______________ news? Mrs Johnson is going to have a baby. **(late)**

f) The ____________ person in Form 9a is Jonathan. He's even ______________ than most of the teachers. **(tall)**

g) We have to be at school by nine o'clock, but usually we get there __________ than that. **(early)**

h) Mandy is trying to get ______________, so she's eating lots of salads and no cake. Soon she'll be the _______________ person in the class. **(thin)**

6. Apostrophe

27. **Apostrophe im Singular und Plural.** Schreibe hinter jeden Ausdruck hin, ob das unterstrichene Wort im Singular (Sg.) oder Plural (Pl.) steht.

Beispiel: the <u>elephant's</u> tail *Sg.* the <u>ladies'</u> room *Pl.*

a) on a <u>summer's</u> day _______ b) rugby <u>players'</u> voices __________

c) the <u>team's</u> captain ________ d) the <u>Lord's</u> prayer _________

e) the <u>women's</u> uniform _______ f) a few <u>weeks'</u> holiday ________

Es sind genauso viele Singular- wie Pluralformen. **Tipp**

28. Setze die Apostrophe.

Kein Apostroph bei *yours, theirs, ours.* **Tipp**

a) Janes dad was looking forward to Wolstanton Mens Choirs trip to see Londons most famous sights. **(4)**

b) After a few minutes the actors and actresses didnt answer any more of this interviewers questions. **(2)**

c) Patricia joined the Womens Institute, where she met a lot of her husbands friends wives. **(3)**

d) There is a birds nest under the Browns roof. **(2)**

e) Tobys dad has got a weeks holiday in May. **(2)**

f) Ill see you in an hours time at St. Annes Square. **(3)**

g) Stephens parents have got the same sort of car as weve got, but theirs is red and ours is black. **(2)**

29. Schreibe den unterstrichenen Teil in der Kurzform.

Beispiel: What is the time? *what's*

a) There is a ghost in the castle. ____________

b) We are going now. ____________

c) They have had lunch. ____________

d) Maria says she will be back soon. ____________

e) I am afraid I cannot help you. ____________

____

f) Do not worry, it will be all right. ____________

____

g) Tom has not gone yet. ____________

h) He will not go till we have had dinner. ____________

____

30. In den folgenden Sätzen fehlen alle Apostrophe. Deine Aufgabe ist es, sie aufzuspüren und einzusetzen.

Tipp Du kannst dir diesen Text auch diktieren lassen.

Todays the first day back at school after the holidays. Daniels teacher is giving some information to her pupils. Therell be a weeks holiday at the beginning of November. On 26th November its the head teachers birthday, and its the choirs job to sing a few songs for him. Next week theres a table tennis tournament, teachers against pupils. Im playing in that, but I dont think Ill win. Youre all too good for me! Oh yes, and the Parents Association wants to hold a jumble sale, so if youve got any old toys, childrens clothes etc., dont forget to bring them in two weeks time. Weve got two football matches against Biddulph High School at the end of October. The girls match is on 29th and the boys match is on 31st, just before the holidays begin. Both matches start at 3 oclock. Id also like to say that some pupils idea of "on time" isnt the same as mine. Id like you to be here at quarter to nine in the morning. If youre late we cant get on with the lessons. You really mustnt forget that. Now, Im organizing the school play this year, and rehearsals begin next month. Ive decided whos playing the detectives part and whos playing the heros part, but there are lots of other characters, so I hope youll come to the casting in a weeks time. Any questions? Well, I think thats all for now. Its nearly ten oclock. Lets get on with the English lesson.

Insgesamt solltest du 41 Apostrophe gesetzt haben. **Tipp**

7. Groß- und Kleinschreibung

31. **Schau den Beispielsatz an und ergänze dann die Regel.**

a) *Wolstanton High School is a nice school in the North of England.*

Wörter, die Teil eines ______________ sind, werden großgeschrieben. (Ausnahme: kleine Wörter wie *of / and / the*)

b) *Most British people only speak English.*

____________namen, auch wenn sie als Adjektiv stehen, werden großgeschrieben.

c) *Where's the house with the apple tree in the garden?*

Sonst werden alle Wörter, auch ________________, kleingeschrieben.

d) *Jasmin always takes her little rucksack to kindergarten.*

Deutsche Nomen, die ins Englische übernommen worden sind, werden wie alle anderen englischen Nomen ____________geschrieben.

e) *Jane's favourite subjects at school are Music and History.*

Schulfächer werden _________geschrieben.

f) *The day after Christmas Day is called Boxing Day.*

Die Namen von ________________________ werden großgeschrieben.

32. **Setze in die Lücken die angegebenen Buchstaben in der vorgegebenen Reihenfolge ein. Entscheide, ob sie groß- oder kleingeschrieben werden.**

a) Lisa is twenty-two. She wants to get a __ob at a __otel. She speaks __rench and __panish and she's travelled quite a lot in __uropean countries. **j – h – f – s – e**

b) Lots of __ourists go to London, especially in the __ummer. They take a __axi or a __us to their __otel. Then they wander around with a __uck-sack on their back and a town __lan in their __and.
t – s - t – b – h – r – p – h

c) A lot of them are __merican, but some __sian or __uropean. They don't usually go to the __orth of __ngland, but if they have time they go to the __cottish Highlands. **a – a – e – n – e – s**

d) In the __outh-__est of __ngland the wind often blows over the __ea from the __est. **s – w – e – s - w**

e) Sarah's __octor is a young man called __r __oung. He's interested in languages and he's learning __urkish. In his holidays he packs a __ucksack and backpacks around __urope for a few weeks.
d – d – y – t – r – e

f) Sarah and her mum and dad are going to the __lack __orest in __ermany for their holidays. Sarah imagines a very dark __orest with __lack trees, but of course, it isn't really like that. **b – f – g – f – b**

g) In __ermany people open their __hristmas __resents on __hristmas __ve. Children in __ritain hang their socks up that __vening. In the morning of __hristmas __ay they get up early and find toys and __hocolate in their socks, and lots of presents under the __hristmas __ree. And the 6th __ecember? It's just a normal __ay – nothing special. **g – c – p – c – e – b – e – c – d – c – c – t – d – d**

33. **Hier gibt's noch einige Übungssätze zur Groß- und Kleinschreibung.**

a) Fabian, Daniel and their friends go to a __chool called Wolstanton __igh __chool in an __ld __treet called – surprise, surprise! – __ld __treet.
s – h – s – o – s – o – s

b) Fabian's favourite subjects are __aths and __eography. He likes playing __ockey in the __inter and __ennis in the __ummer.
m – g – h – w – t – s

c) Iris and Caroline did a __roject about __obs. They interviewed other children. Some girls wanted to be __indergarten teachers, a few boys wanted to be __otor mechanics, one girl wanted to be a __ockey and two of the boys wanted to be __armers. One boy's dream was to be a professional footballer and play in the __orld __up.
p – j – k – m – j – f – w – c

d) Paul has made a __onster out of __and. It's a __haracter out of a __ilm.
m – s – c – f

e) A lot of people don't go to the __ank these days. They use a __omputer to manage their money.
b – c

f) One of England's most famous __ings was __ing Alfred the __reat.
k – k – g

g) The __ueen __other had her 100th birthday on 4th August 2000. She was __een Elizabeth's __other.
q – m – q – m

8. Zusammen- und Getrenntschreibung

34. Zusammen oder getrennt? Bedenke: Jedes Wort hat **nur eine** Betonung. Unterstreiche die betonten Silben in diesen Kombinationen.

Beispiel: football History lesson

a) sweatshirt b) blackboard c) post office
d) holidaymaker e) cake factory f) Christmas party
g) own goal h) cricket match

35. Diese Sätze sind zusammengeschrieben; nur die Betonungen werden mit Fettdruck auf den betonten Vokalen angegeben. Setze die Wortgrenzen.

Beispiel: J**e**ff's|d**a**d|is|a|p**o**stman. His|br**o**ther|has|got|a|h**o**liday|j**o**b|in|a|c**a**ke|f**a**ctory.

a) Therearel**o**tsofh**o**lidaymakersintheBl**a**ckF**o**restin thes**u**mmerh**o**lidays.

b) Inthel**a**stf**oo**tballm**a**tchF**a**bianssc**o**redan**o**wng**oa**l.

c) St**e**phenandT**o**byareg**o**ingtost**a**yinay**ou**thh**o**stel andd**o**as**i**ghtseeingt**ou**rofL**o**ndon.

d) They'rep**a**ckingsw**ea**tshirtsandp**u**lloversintheir r**u**cksacks.

e) There'sasch**oo**ltr**i**psotherearel**o**tsofsch**oo**lchildren atthem**ai**nentr**a**nceofthesch**oo**l.

f) Thesch**oo**lb**u**sist**a**kingthemtother**ai**lwayst**a**tion.

g) T**o**byisaveget**a**riansohew**o**n'tbeeatingb**a**con s**a**ndwichesandh**o**td**o**gslikehiscl**a**ssmates.

h) Theywillbetr**a**vellingonthe**u**nderground.

i) H**o**wdoesthet**i**cketmach**i**new**o**rk?

Tipp

Diese Anzahl der Wörter (in anderer Reihenfolge) müsstest du in deinen Sätzen am Ende haben: 8 – 10 – 10 – 7 – 13 – 18 –17 – 17– 6.

36. Aus wie vielen Wörtern bestehen diese Kombinationen? Schreibe die Zahl hin.

Beispiele:	Christmas	party		2
	foot	ball	match	2
	school	bus	stop	3

a)	cricket	match		______
b)	down	stairs	toilet	______
c)	base	ball	team	______
d)	some	thing		______
e)	news	paper	article	______
f)	class	mate		______
g)	bath	room	door	______
h)	main	entrance	hall	______
i)	sight	seeing	tour	______
j)	taxi	driver		______
k)	scrap	book		______

Tipp

Wenn du deine Ergebnisse a) – k) addierst, müsste die Summe 20 betragen.

37. Diese erfundenen E-Mail-Adressen haben weder Wortgrenzen noch Apostrophe. Schreibe die Namen, die du dahinter vermutest, in normaler Schrift hin. Es sind Namen, daher müssen sie großgeschrieben werden.

Beispiel: johnsplanet@imagine.com — John's Planet

a) castletennisclub@guess.where ______________

b) davescafe@… ______________

c) beachhotel@… ______________

d) 3oclockbar@… ______________

e) allsaintschurch@… ______________

f) annescheeseshop@… ______________

g) tomstaxis@… ______________

9. Unbetonte Silben, Wortendungen und -anfänge

38. Unbetonte und stumme Silben können beim Diktat ein Problem darstellen. Kreise bei diesen 2-silbigen Wörtern die unbetonten Silben ein.

r u g b y	j e w e l	c o r r e c t	a u t u m n
d e s i g n	d i v o r c e d	d o c t o r	a b o u t
s l o g a n	l i t t l e	m u s t n ' t	c a r e f u l

39. Ergänze die Wörter (der Laut ist immer [ə]):

a) Asi___ ['eɪʃə]	b) shelt___ ['ʃeltə]	c) driv___ ['draɪvə]
d) camer___ ['kæmərə]	e) mot___ ['məʊtə]	f) smuggl___ ['smʌglə]
g) met___ ['mi:tə]	h) visit___ ['vɪzɪtə]	i) act___ ['æktə]
j) fig___ ['fɪgə]	k) popul___ ['pɒpjələ]	l) eith___ ['aɪðə]
m) advent___ [əd'ventʃə]	n) calend___ ['kælɪndə]	

40. Ergänze mit *-ous* oder *-ess.*

a) delici___	b) nerv___	c) actr___	d) danger___
e) religi___	f) fam___	g) waitr___	

41. Unterstreiche die Wörter, die mit *-ent* enden, und ergänze die Endung bei den übrigen.

pres❄	restaur❄	brilli❄	eleph❄
assist❄	accid❄	import❄	par❄
differ❄	pavem❄		

42. Wortendungen, die [ɪt] / [ɪd] ausgesprochen werden.

a) Füge die fünf verschiedenen Endungen wieder ein. Sie klingen alle ähnlich, jedoch nicht gleich.

Have you heard the stup_ _ story of the ghost rabb_ _ in the haunt_ _ house oppos_ _ _ the crick_ _ ground?

b) Ergänze die Wörter.

jack___ favour___ pack___ hundr___

helm___ toil___ tick___ supermark___

Tipp

Eine der drei vorkommenden Endungen ist mit sechs Stück klar in der Überzahl.

43. Diesen Wörtern fehlen die Anfänge. Es kommen *de-*, *dis-* und *di-* vor. Schreibe die passende Anfangssilbe hin.

a) _dis_cuss b) _____scribe c) _____tective

d) _____vorced e) _____cussion f) _____abled

g) _____licious h) _____cide i) _____appear

j) _____sign

44. Diese Wörter haben am Anfang ein unbetontes [ə]. Ergänze.

a) ___cross b) ___ssistant c) ___pinion d) ___ntil

45. Doppel- oder Einzelkonsonant? Ergänze die fehlenden Buchstaben in den Wörtern. Sie sind alle vorgegeben. Ein Eindringling hat sich allerdings eingeschlichen. Welcher ist es?

s – b – s – r – r – s – g – s – b – d – r – d – p – d – r – g – p – c – g

a) a___istant b) a___ross c) a___o d) a___ear

e) a___venture f) a___ainst g) a___ound h) a___ive

i) a___ove j) a___ree k) a___ress l) a___road

m) a___embly

46. **Der Laut [əʊ], wie in *window, disco.***
Harry, Phil und Bob sind drei Dorfpolizisten, die einen Raub aufklären mussten. Jeder schrieb einen Teil des Berichts, aber nur einer hat die Rechtschreibung überprüft.
Deine detektivischen Aufgaben:

a) Welcher Polizist hat die Rechtschreibung überprüft? ____________

b) Korrigiere die Rechtschreibfehler der anderen zwei (es handelt sich nur um unbetontes [əʊ] am Wortende).

c) Welcher Polizist schrieb die Einkaufsliste *(shopping list)*? __________

Harry: We had to follow the robbers down narrow streets to a little village. Their herow, a man they call Beard, owns a discow there.
Phil: Beard was looking out of the windo. We think that he was also listening to the radio. We took a photo of him.
Bob: We also got a photo of the robbers, but we couldn't follow them into the house. The passage was very narrow. It was also quite dark, and none of us wanted to be a hero, so we used our radio to ask for help.

47. **Zu jeder Gruppe von Wortteilen passt ein bestimmter Anfang. Ordne richtig zu. Allerdings gibt es zwei Eindringlinge, die nirgendwohin passen.**

com- com- per- pre- to- to- con- ex- ex- ~~ex~~- un- un- re- re-

a) *ex* ____ -plain -change -ample
b) ______ -cord -port -ceive -turn
c) ______ -pare -puter
d) ______ -press -pensive
e) ______ -gether -night -day
f) ______ -friendly -lucky
g) ______ -pare -sent
h) ______ -member -ligious -peat

i)	_______ -wards	-morrow
j)	_______-bine	-plete
k)	_______-cuse	-citing
l)	_______ -til	-happy

Die Eindringlinge: __________ __________

48. Jetzt kannst du Wortendungen andocken. Zwei passen nirgendwo-hin. Welche sind es diesmal?

-ful -ish -er -ic -age -age -tion

-ful -ish -ic -ic -ice -age -ive

a)	com-	mus-	top-	______
b)	mess-	gar-		______
c)	care-	beauti-		______
d)	expens-	detect-		______
e)	rubb-	Turk-		______
f)	electr-	ethn-		______
g)	serv-	off-	not-	______
h)	man-	langu-		______
i)	traff-	authent-		______
j)	wonder-	use-		______
k)	Span-	fin-		______
l)	vill-	saus-		______

Die beiden Irrläufer: __________ __________

49. Unbetontes [l] / [əl]: Ergänze mit vier verschiedenen Endungen.

Some of Mr Norton's pup__s trav__ to school by bus. Others cyc__. The school is quite near the hospit__.

50. **Welche Wörter werden gesucht? Lies den Hinweis links durch und schreibe dann das Wort rechts hin.**

Tipp

Die Wörter enden alle mit dem Laut [l] oder [əl].

a) a sort of fruit: *apple*
b) a month of the year: __ p __ __ __
c) the opposite of big: __ i __ __ __ __
d) it's made of wax, and gives light: c __ __ d __ __
e) one person, but a lot of: __ __ o __ __ __
f) general word for a hamster, an elephant: __ n __ m __ __
g) it's got two wheels and it hasn't got an engine: __ i __ y c __ __
h) to make a tune by blowing through your lips: __ h __ s t __ __
i) a parent's brother: __ n __ __ __

THWELIS – LOPEEP – CLUNE – ~~PALPE~~ – DALCEN – CILBECY – MAILAN – TELLIT – PIRAL

51. **Schreibe Wörter aus diesem Text neben die entsprechenden deutschen Wörter. Die Reihenfolge stimmt.**

… You can camp, or stay at a hotel or youth hostel. Enjoy the magical atmosphere in Smugglers' Cove. No need to take your car – you can hire a bicycle or travel by bus. Visit the old castle on Strawberry Hill. Treat yourself to *(gönnen Sie sich)* a candle-lit dinner in the central part of town, with classical music and some local wine. (Check the label on the bottle!) Or sit at a table outside, for a traditional meal of fish and chips at a seaside pub. Join in the local festivals. Find unusual souvenirs, including jewellery made from real sea shells, in the little shops on the sea front. Looking for friendly people and beautiful scenery? This is the place to come!

Herberge *hostel*
zauberhaft __ __ __ __ __ __ 12
Schmuggler __ __ 10 __ __ __ __ __ __ ’
Fahrrad 4 __ __ __ __ __ __
reisen __ __ __ __ __ 5

Burg	_ _ _ 7 _ _
Kerze	_ _ _ 1 _ _
zentral	_ _ _ _ 8 _ _
klassisch	_ _ _ _ _ _ _ _ _
Etikett	_ _ _ _ _
Flasche	11 _ _ _ _ _
Tisch	_ _ _ _ _
traditionell	_ _ _ _ _ _ _ 9 _ _ _
Gericht (Essen)	_ _ _ _
Fest	_ _ _ _ _ _ _ _ _
ungewöhnlich	_ _ _ _ _ _ _
Schmuck	_ _ _ 6 _ _ _ _ _
echt	_ _ _ _
klein	_ _ _ _ _ 13
Leute	_ _ 2 _ _ _
wunderschön	_ _ _ 3 _ _ _ _ _

Das Lösungswort ist eine Bezeichnung für Zwillinge:

_ _ _ _ _ _ _ _ _ _ _ _ _ _ !

52. Folgende Endungen fehlen den Wörtern unten. Ergänze sie.

-an -en -on -ine -ion

Tipp

Es handelt sich immer um die Laute [n] / [ən] / [ɪn].

a) eng___ b) giv___ c) conversat___ d) bac___

e) forgott___ f) happ___ g) express___ h) Europe___

i) Asi___ j) kitch___ k) Indi___ l) op___

53. **Die fehlenden Wörter findest du in der Lautschrift. Schreibe sie richtig hin.**

a) A ___________ is a small green or blue bird. People keep them in cages. ['bʌdʒi]

b) Ice ___________ is a game played with sticks and a puck on ice. ['hɒki]

c) A box with nothing in it is an __________________ box. ['empti]

d) If you don't know a word, you can look it up in a __________________. ['dɪkʃənəri]

e) People often drink a cup of tea or ______________ in the morning. ['kɒfi]

f) You can hire a car with a driver at most railway stations. It's called a _______. ['tæksi]

g) When you travel a long way, you make a __________________. ['dʒɜːni]

h) Lots of people go to church on _______________ morning. ['sʌndi]

i) Another word for "perhaps" is "_______________" ['meibi]

Tipp

Ist dir aufgefallen, dass alle diese Wörter am Ende den Laut [i] haben, aber trotzdem unterschiedlich geschrieben werden?

54. **Daniel musste als Hausaufgabe ein Märchen schreiben. Darin kamen viele Wörter mit stummen Konsonanten vor. Unterstreiche die betreffenden Buchstaben.**

Once upon a time there was a princess, the daughter of a powerful king. She lived on an island in a big castle. Her life was very boring. She wasn't allowed to go for walks outside the garden, and there was nobody to talk to. She could whistle like a bird, but she knew that ladies shouldn't do that. Now, one rainy night in autumn, there came a knock at the door …

Tipp

Zähle die Stellen, wo stummen Konsonanten vorkommen (z.B. *whistle* = 2 Stellen, *night* = 1 Stelle). Die Zahl der Stellen ist eine Primzahl zwischen 10 und 20.

55. Diesen Wörtern fehlen Vokale, die man in der gesprochenen Sprache nicht hört. Schreibe sie korrekt aus. Welcher Buchstabe in der Liste bleibt übrig?

ev◇rybody	______________	que◇◇	______________
su◇table	______________	fru◇t	______________
bisc◇it	______________	dialog◇◇	______________
fright◇ning	______________	nat◇◇nal	______________

e – e – e – e – i – i – i – i – o - u – u – u

Übrig bleibt _______.

56. In jeder Reihe werden die unterstrichenen Vokallaute mehr oder weniger gleich ausgesprochen – außer bei einem Wort in der Reihe. Finde in jeder Reihe das Wort, das nicht passt.

done – above – front – bone – worry 1
enough – south - jump – none – rucksack 2
soon – sun – son – study – other 3
smuggle – some – supermarket – love – up 4
Monday – Sunday – fun – come – alone 5
uncle – unit – under – unhappy – London 6

authentic – draw – forest – horse – born 7
tall – autumn – before – below – saw 8
actor – board – also – talk – caught 9

wet – head – healthy – said – mean 10
meant – red – even – ever – sweatshirt 11

interview – uniform – study – rescue – queue 12

youth – young – stupid – usual – statue 13

shoe – proof – improve – lose – both 14

rule – food – above – include – two 15

south – souvenir – suitable – roof – do 16

journey – turn – tour – learn – bird 17

sure – person – Turkish – girl – nervous 18

return – service – dear – work – burn 19

European – dialogue – hero – receive – metre 20

mind – type – why – pilot – repeat 21

find – eye – island – skiing – diary 22

great – age – ago – explain – exchange 23

manage – maybe – Asian – disabled – label 24

eight – tail – language – conversation – bacon 25

In diesem Witz stehen die Ziffern für die Nummern der Reihen oben. Füge den ersten Buchstaben des Wortes ein, das du als unpassend identifiziert hast, um den Witz lesen zu können.

A woman woke her husband up and said, "there's a 24-5 n in the kitchen. He's eating the 14-i-2c-6-i-17-4 I made to20-9-13. Phone the 11-10-e-21-gency 3ervice18!"
"Who 16-h-9-l-25 I 23-22-k 7or?" said her husband, "police or 15-10-1-6-25-9-nc-11?"

57. Ergänze die unvollständigen Wörter. Der Laut [s] fehlt. Die jeweils richtigen Vorschläge (rechts) helfen dir, den Witz unten zu vervollständigen. (Die Reihenfolge stimmt.)

a)	Iris's mum gave her a loving ki__	ss: C	s: W
	before she left the hou__.	s: I	se: A
b)	Mahatma Ghandi was a famou__	se: L	s: N
	religiou__ leader.	ce: L	s: T
c)	Louis Pasteur was a __ientist.	sc: M	s: S
d)	Wait for me at the main entran__.	ce: A	se: E
e)	Broken gla__	s: E	ss: D
	can be dangerou__.	se: N	s: E

f)	Iris's dad and mum are divor__d.	ce: M	se: T
g)	Her dad is going out with somebody el__, now.	ce: O	se: I
h)	If there's an accident, call an ambulan__.	ce: S	se: U
i)	When a hor__ puts its ears back,	se: T	s: R
	that means it's nervou__.	se: I	s: A
j)	Jane doesn't like 'true or fal__?'	s: S	se: K
	exer__ises.	s: T	c: E

JOKE: Ann and Becky were having a day out in the countryside. Suddenly Ann stopped, and said: "This is a lovely place for a picnic."

"You're right," answered Becky. "After all, five hundred thousand ants *(Ameisen)*

__ __ __' __ have __ __ __ __ a __ __ __ __ __ __ __".

58. In diesem Text fehlt der Laut [tʃ] wie in *chair* oder *watch.* Ergänze mit *-ch-* bzw *-tch-.*

Jane's dad is wa___ing a tennis ma___ on TV. He and Alfie are ex___anging their opinions on the game. Jane is making a ___art for homework, and her mum is making a ___eese cake in the ki___en.

"Can you rea___ the sugar for me, Jane? I haven't got mu___ time, because I want to go to ___ur___."

"Sure. Whi___ one, brown or white?"

"I don't mind. You ___oose."

Insgesamt gehören 27 Buchstaben hinein. **Tipp**

59. Der Laut [ʃ]. Jane hat gerade eine Brieffreundschaft mit einem japanischen Mädchen angefangen. Das Mädchen hat zurückgeschrieben. Schreibe die unvollständigen Wörter aus.

Dear Jane,

Thank you for your letter. My Engli++ ______________ isn't very good, I have to use a dic++onary _______________ for lots of words and expre+++ons ________________. But I'm +ure ___________ I ++all

_____________ improve. You say that you like tradi++onal __________________ A++an _______________ foods like rice and fi++ __________. I do, too, but my mother says I eat too much +ugar ______________. ++e ___________ says I'm getting fat. My favourite food is chocolate ice cream. Deli++ous _______________! Is it true that the na++onal ____________ sport of the Briti++ ___________ people is foot-ball? I must fini++ _____________ now. Best wi++es ___________ to you and your parents, Love, Mao.

60. **Hier fehlen die Buchstaben, die den Laut [ks] repräsentieren. Schreibe sie in die Lücken.**

a) for e◯ample b) e◯ercise c) e◯change

d) ta◯i e) e◯iting f) e◯plain

g) a◯ident h) ne◯t

Tipp Insgesamt fehlen 10 Buchstaben.

61. Hier fehlen **unbetonte Vokale**. **Füge sie wieder ein.**

a) In the aut__mn term, the school choir starts practising for the Christm__s conc__rt.

b) To get to the school off__ce, go through the main entr__nce and take the first corr__dor on the right.

a – a – e – i – i – u

c) Jane would like to study langu__ges. She knows some French and a bit of Germ__n.

d) Mr Norton is org__nizing a skiing trip for Form 8a. They're looking forward to the mount__ns and for__sts in Austria.

e) Toby is looking forward to the airp__rt, and his vegetari__n meal on the plane. He would like to talk to the pil__t, too.

a – a – a – a – a - e – i – o – o

f) Iris is going to bring back some snow in a bottle as a souv__nir. She doesn't like the things tour__sts us__lly buy.

g) Everybody is looking in their cupb__rds at home for warm clothes. Fabian is going to buy some new gloves at his fav__rite sports shop, opp__site the post office.

a – a – e – i – o – o – o – u – u

62. *Word search*

Die Wörter laufen in folgenden Richtungen: → ↗ ↘ ↓
Jedes Wort schließt sich einem anderen an.

N	R	W	T	E	O	Z	S	Y	B	J	C	A	Y	P	J	K	Q
O	Q	A	U	T	U	M	N	M	I	B	O	A	U	E	M	Y	K
E	F	H	O	Q	A	M	I	U	J	X	I	Z	S	A	I	C	V
P	B	W	T	Y	C	L	I	M	B	A	Y	U	W	T	S	R	D
L	T	H	D	B	C	I	K	F	N	C	X	G	Y	F	L	W	I
K	N	O	W	B	S	C	X	T	B	F	N	A	B	B	A	E	X
N	Z	N	A	J	O	H	D	V	R	I	Q	D	R	E	N	N	L
J	G	F	L	N	I	R	K	M	E	W	S	P	L	L	D	F	W
B	H	W	K	S	G	I	X	E	V	H	P	C	V	L	J	D	R
A	X	X	A	H	S	S	S	A	E	I	K	U	U	Z	R	L	I
N	T	C	M	S	O	T	X	G	R	E	H	O	F	I	V	Z	T
V	D	L	W	I	H	M	V	D	Y	Q	W	H	I	S	T	L	E
H	H	L	H	G	I	A	M	U	W	H	G	A	A	I	N	J	U
B	M	P	I	N	K	S	D	Z	H	Y	D	Q	U	L	Y	U	R
E	L	S	R	S	Z	J	C	G	E	Q	E	R	O	Q	V	V	V
T	R	T	K	P	T	S	K	W	R	S	F	M	F	E	O	E	Z
O	P	G	G	W	E	E	Q	U	E	U	E	K	S	O	A	C	S
L	T	S	C	C	N	I	N	T	K	C	Q	P	G	G	U	F	B

1. ['krɪsməs] is celebrated on 25th December.
2. Spring, summer, ['ɔ:təm], winter.
3. Toby [wʊd] like to be in the school football team
4. Wenn du in mein Zimmer willst, … you should [nɒk] on the door.

5. If you want to see the sights, go on a ['saɪtsi:ɪŋ] tour.
6. Wenn du einen Brief geschrieben hast, … you [sain] your name at the end.
7. A line of people waiting in a shop or at the cinema is called a [kju:].
8. Apples, oranges and bananas are all types of [fru:t].
9. If you've lost your voice, you can't sing, but you can ['wɪsl].
10. Some people [wɔ:k] to school, others cycle.
11. The town centre is very crowded on Saturdays. There are people ['evriweə].
12. The sea is all around Britain. It's an ['aɪlənd].
13. This is a ['kɑ:sl]

14. People often eat a ['bɪskɪt] with their coffee.
15. Do you [nəʊ] where Andy is? I can't find him.
16. Babies start to [tɔ:k] when they're about two years old.
17. Wenn jemand ganz leise spricht, ... you have to ['lɪsən] very carefully.
18. Somebody [hu:] flies a plane is called a pilot.
19. One, [tu:], three, four ...
20. Little boys love to [klaɪm] up into trees.
21. You can either phone your friends, or you can [raɪt] e-mails to them.
22. Du willst einen Kuchen unter zwei Personen aufteilen, ... so you cut it into two [hɑ:vz].

D Übungsdiktate 1

Einige Hinweise für den Vorleser oder die Vorleserin:

Wörter, deren Aussprache mithilfe der Lautschrift oder des Betonungsmusters dargestellt wird, sind mit einem (*) gekennzeichnet. **Betonungsmuster** stellen die betonte Silbe mit einem **O** dar und unbetonte Silben mit einem **o**, zum Beispiel: *imagine* = oOo. In der Lautschrift wird die betonte Silbe durch einen [ˈ] davor angezeigt, zum Beispiel: *opinion* = [əˈpɪnjən]. Sprechpausen werden bei Punkt und Komma gemacht, zusätzliche Sprechpausen werden durch ein (ˈ) kenntlich gemacht. Punkt = *full stop*, Komma = *comma*; Semikolon = *semicolon* [semiˈkəʊlən]; Anführungszeichen = *quotation marks*; Gedankenstrich = *dash*; Doppelpunkt = *colon*

1. Pluralformen

Tante Paula und Onkel Fred machen eine Kreuzfahrt. Hier ist ein Brief von Paula an Fabian und seine Familie.

We are enjoying our trip. As you know, I don't like plane journeys*, ['dʒɜ:niz]
and if you take the car ˈ you always have to ˈ study maps etc. I like
boats ˈ best of all. I must say ˈ there are some strange characters ˈ on
board the ship, but it's mainly the men. Their wives ˈ are really nice
people. It isn't boring here, anyway; there are lots of activities,
and there are ˈ some good programmes ˈ on TV. I watch ˈ all the
tennis matches, but nothing else. Yesterday we stopped ˈ on the
south coast ˈ of France. I didn't like it – too many factories and
docks, and not enough nice beaches. I will write again soon.
Love and kisses, Paula.

(114 words)

2. Pluralformen

Noch ein Brief von Tante Paula.

The trouble with holidays is ˈ that there are ˈ too many tourists ˈ
in the cities. Yesterday we put our rucksacks ˈ on our backs ˈ
and went off into Naples*. There are store detectives ˈ in the big [neɪplz]
shops, and I'm sure ˈ half the people ˈ who live there ˈ are smugglers.
We tried to phone for a taxi ˈ but the telephones didn't seem to work,
and we couldn't understand ˈ the bus timetables. We had some good
pizzas, and the waiters and waitresses were friendly. They spoke English,
so we didn't need our dictionaries*. We saw some beautiful churches. Oooo
And you should see the tomatoes ˈ in big boxes ˈ at the markets here.
Better than the ones at home! Love and best wishes, Paula and Fred.

(119 words)

3. Pluralformen

Figures* show | that a lot of young people | have road accidents | ['fɪgəz]
on the way home from discos. Some even lose their lives. They
have often had | a few glasses of beer, and they feel like heroes,
so they drive too fast. It's a big problem, because taxis are expensive |
and buses don't usually* | run at night. There is a new service | in ['ju:ʒʊəlɪ]
some cities, where you can buy cheap taxi tickets. If three or four
young men and women* | take a taxi together, none of them | ['wɪmɪn]
has to pay very much.
(91 words)

4. Dritte Person Singular (-s)

More and more German people | are coming to the area | where
Fabian lives. There is a new German club | in the nearest large town.
The programme includes* walks, cycle rides, film evenings etc. oO
Sometimes Fabian's dad goes to a club meeting | and discusses
ideas | for new events with his friends. The discussion finishes |
at half past nine, but he often reaches home | at eleven or later.
He stays at the pub | because he enjoys speaking German | with
other adults*. ['ædʌlts]
(77 words)

5. Dritte Person Singular

There is a funny man in the German club. He scares Jasmin,
Fabian's little sister, because he has a very loud voice. He swings
his arms | when he walks, and sometimes Fabian follows him |
and copies the way he walks. There is also a young woman |
who studies Geography* and flies off | to different parts [dʒɪ'ɒgrəfɪ] oOoo
of the world. She likes Fabian, and sometimes sends him a
postcard. One of the ladies in the club | is a student.
She teaches German at Fabian's school. In the club he calls
her Ute, but at school | he tries to call her Miss Graf.
(100 words)

6. *-ing* und *-ed* Formen des Verbs

The children in Form 9a | have been planning a project | on power.
One group is organizing posters | showing how people are
improving* the situation | with windmills, wave power etc. [ɪm'pru:vɪŋ]
They are cutting out photos | from magazines, copying
articles and drawing pictures. Another group is preparing
an experiment | to show how wind power works. The teacher
has explained it to them | and they have copied the notes |
from the blackboard. Mr May studied Physics and Geography |
when he was younger, and he has travelled abroad a lot.
The two groups are exchanging information. Does the wind
power experiment work? Yes! Everybody is clapping. The
children are having a great time.

(109 words)

7. Steigerung der Adjektive auf *-er* und *-est* und Adverbien

Caroline has changed completely. Two years ago, she was
one of the shortest girls | in the class, and she was fatter |
than most kids of her age. Now she has become taller and
thinner. She's fitter and healthier, too. She eats less sugar
than before, and more salad. Two years ago she could only
run slowly. In fact, she was the slowest in the class. Now she
can run eight kilometres* quite easily, and more quickly than ['kɪləmi:təz]
some of her classmates. She feels better, too, and it's easier
to find clothes* that fit her. She says C and A have the nicest, [kləʊ(ð)z]
cheapest clothes.

(104 words)

8. Adjektive und Adverbien

Fabian and Paul have got a younger sister | called Jasmin. When
Jasmin was five she started school. "What will it be like?", she
asked nervously.
"Well," said Paul, "I know you're a big girl now, but most of the
children | at school | will be bigger than you, because they're older.
I hope you get Mrs Wild. She's the kindest teacher at the school.
She's got the noisiest class. She lets the children move* around freely. [mu:v]
Wait until she reads you a story. She does it wonderfully. She makes
the scary bits even scarier, and the nice bits even nicer. If you ask her,
she'll draw a picture specially* for you." ['speʃlɪ]

(112 words)

9. Der Apostroph

Some of the boys and girls in Form 9a ˈ already know ˈ what they'd like to do ˈ when they're grown up. A few of the boys want to be pilots, and one or two want to be detectives. A pilot's job isn't easy, but Robert, for example, is sure he'll be able to do it. He's working hard at school ˈ to get the marks he needs. The girls' ideas are different. Two of them want to be actresses* ˈ and one wants to ['æktrəsɪz] work ˈ in a ladies' clothes shop. Mandy can't imagine a life ˈ without horses, and she's sure that she'll have her own riding school ˈ one day.
(106 words)

10. Der Apostroph

It's four o'clock on Friday afternoon. Jane's mum is doing the week's shopping. Jane and Alfie are helping her. But where's Alfie? He's not here. There he is, looking at the children's comics. "You're terrible", Jane says. "You really mustn't run off. No, don't put the comics in the basket, I'm sure Mum won't want to buy them for you. Anyway, this isn't ours, it's another lady's basket. You must leave other people's things alone. Look, let's buy some chocolate* biscuits*. You choose yours and I'll choose mine. ['tʃɒklət] ['bɪskɪts] These ones in the red packets are the nicest. There's lots of chocolate on the outside ˈ and biscuit in the middle."
(109 words)

11. Apostroph und Groß- und Kleinschreibung

Dear Mandy,
I'm writing from the Queen's Hotel. We're just staying here for one night ˈ on our way to Wales, because it's more ˈ than one day's journey. I've seen cars ˈ from lots of different countries – French ones, Italian ones, and even one American car. This is a good hotel ˈ and the owner's daughter ˈ is the same age as me. We've been playing ˈ computer games together. That's not my parents' idea ˈ of a healthy activity, but I don't care. My new friend goes riding ˈ at a place ˈ where smugglers lived years ago. It's called Smugglers' Hill Farm. Her horse's name is Fred. It's a boy's name, but the horse is a girl. Love, Caroline.
(113 words)

12. Groß- und Kleinschreibung

Jasmin has left kindergarten now. She goes to a real school. Most
of the kids in her class are British, but there are some Asian
children, one Turkish boy ˈ and some children ˈ from other
European* countries. Jasmin is the only German child in [jʊərəˈpiːən] – ooOo
the class. The class is practising for the Christmas* play. [ˈkrɪsməs]
There are lots of characters, including farmers, animals and
kings. Jasmin is a king. Her brothers call her King Jasmin now,
as a joke. Her dad is going to record* the play on film. [rɪˈkɔːd] – oO

(87 words)

13. Ein Wort oder zwei?

Everybody is talking about ˈ the next school holidays. Robert has
got a new mountain bike ˈ for his birthday, so he'll be riding
around ˈ on farm tracks and country roads. Daniel has been
looking in the newspaper ˈ for a holiday job, but he hasn't found
anything yet. Fabian's uncle and aunt are coming for a week,
so Fabian and his brother are going ˈ to take them on a sightseeing
tour ˈ of the nearest big city. Only Iris is quiet*. She wanted to go ˈ [ˈkwaɪət]
on a cycling tour with Jane, and stay at youth hostels, but their
parents said ˈ they were much too young.

(102 words)

14. Ein Wort oder zwei?

Iris and her mum are in the town centre. They've been to the
supermarket ˈ for chocolate biscuits, ice cream and orange juice*, [dʒuːs]
because Iris is having a little birthday party ˈ for six of her
classmates. They've been to a clothes shop, too. Iris has got
two new sweatshirts ˈ and a pullover, and her mum has bought
her ˈ a scrapbook* for her collection of postcards. Now they're Oo
waiting for the bus ˈ outside the shoe shop.

(74 words)

15. Ein Wort oder zwei?

Sarah was at the bus stop, too. Her dad was having trouble ˈ with three big shopping bags ˈ and Sarah's wheelchair, so Iris took a bag from him.
"Thanks," he says, "I almost dropped that one."
"That's all right," said Iris. "Sarah, would you like to come to my party?"
"I'd love that," said Sarah. "Look, here's the bus. Isn't that the bus driver ˈ who sometimes drives your school bus?"
(69 words)

16. Unbetonte Silben

Paul's teacher wants to make the lessons interesting, so she
has organized a visit ˈ to the fire station for her class. Paul has
always wanted to be a hero ˈ and rescue* somebody ˈ from a ['reskju:] Oo
dangerous* situation, so he's very excited about the visit. Ooo
Perhaps he'll be able ˈ to meet some real heroes. At the fire
station, a man called Mr King ˈ shows them lots of yellow
jackets* and helmets. Those are the men's uniforms. And ['dʒækɪts]
the firemen really do slide down ˈ a metal pipe into the
garage*. Paul is surprised about that. He thought it was ['gæra:ʒ] / ['gærɪdʒ]
just a joke.
(99 words)

17. Unbetonte Silben

The fireman who is showing them everything ˈ explains
about different sorts of emergencies*. Sometimes they have oOoo
to go out ˈ to a forest fire, but that's unusual in England ˈ
because of the weather. More often it's a factory ˈ or somebody's
kitchen*. They often have to go to a road ['kɪtʃɪn]
accident*, together with an ambulance. Sometimes ['æksɪdənt] Ooo
they rescue cats from trees, but the fireman says that, in his
opinion, cats can always get down ˈ without help. Their owners
are just too nervous*. Oo
(80 words)

18. Unbetonte Silben

Jane has got an important date in her diary, and she has put
a cross ˈ on the family calendar*, too. She is going to sing ˈ in ['kælɪndə] Ooo
the Christmas concert. The choir* practises twice a week. They're ['kwaɪə]
singing some religious songs, including a few from other nations.
One group of children ˈ is going to act out a play. Daniel is one
of the main actors. There has been a competition to think of a
suitable* slogan ˈ for this year's concert. The winning slogan is ['su:təbl]
"A journey around the world". The concert is very popular, so
almost everybody will be there: mothers, fathers, grandparents
and even a few uncles, aunts and cousins. Jane is already getting
nervous!

(115 words)

19. Unbetonte Silben

Toby and Robert are in the school hockey team. There is often
a game ˈ at another school ˈ at the weekend. There are eleven
players in a team, but usually about fifteen people meet ˈ on the
pavement ˈ outside the main entrance ˈ of the school ˈ on a Saturday
morning ˈ to travel to another village or town. There is a lot of talk ˈ
about right wings, centre halves* and the twenty-three metre line – [hɑ:vz]
hockey players seem to have a language ˈ of their own. They've all
got lunch packets ˈ in their rucksacks. Robert is hoping ˈ that his
mum has packed his favourite bacon sandwiches* ˈ and some ['sænwɪdʒəz]
chocolate biscuits.

(104 words)

20. Stumme Konsonanten

Every autumn* there is a competition ˈ to design Christmas cards. [ɔ:təm]
The designs are on notice boards ˈ in the school hall. One shows
Santa Claus ˈ climbing* high up onto the roof ˈ of a house. In [klaɪmɪŋ]
another one, he is knocking on a door. One girl has done a
card ˈ with famous sights of London ˈ in winter. There is also a
beautiful scene ˈ of a castle on a lonely island. Nobody seems to
know who has done it. Jane is looking at it ˈ and listening to two
people ˈ talking behind her. They're saying ˈ that it is a lovely picture,
but that it has nothing to do with Christmas.

(106 words)

21. Einzel- / Doppelkonsonanten

Iris's dad has been studying marketing. He wants to change his job. It's boring in an office; he would like to travel around the country ˈ and sell clothes with famous labels. He has already had a few interviews. He dressed carefully in his best jacket and tie. Iris is worried. Perhaps he will forget about her ˈ if he's travelling all the time, or if he disappears to the opposite end of Britain. He has been to some places ˈ that look very far away ˈ on the map.

(86 words)

22. Einzel- / Doppelkonsonanten

Iris was spending the weekend with her father. They were out for a picnic ˈ near a forest. Iris wanted to discuss her opinions ˈ with him. It wasn't an easy topic, and Iris had to be careful. When they finished eating ˈ she asked:

"Dad, what will happen if you move away? Will you still come and visit me?"

"Well, I suppose* I won't see you so often," he said. "But we can oO
send e-mails, and there's always the telephone."

"Dad, I want to give you a few tips. I've cut out some articles ˈ from the Wolstanton News, and I've copied some addresses. Please study them first."

(105 words)

23. Alphabet; *false friends*

A new boy has come to the school. His name is Gary Jarvis,
that's G A R Y, J A R V I S*. He's much older than the kids [dʒiː] [eɪ] [ɑː] [waɪ]
in Year 9, and he's very cool. He plays basketball for the [dʒeɪ] [eɪ] [ɑː] [viː]
British team, and he has appeared in a sports quiz ˈ on TV. [aɪ] [es]
They say he owns ten pairs ˈ of sports shoes. He has a good figure, and he's tall, with dark hair and blue eyes. Hundreds of girls are wild about him, and try to meet him ˈ "by chance" in the corridors. Mandy has already had a conversation with him. She says he's a really nice person.

(101 words)

24. Im Deutschen und Englischen ähnliche Wörter

If you believe | that an authentic* top basketball player | can [ɔ:'θentɪk] oOo
lead a normal life | at a school like Wolstanton High, well,
you'll have to think again. Everybody knew | what he was
studying: Technology* in combination with Maths. He had oOoo
little plastic flags on his rucksack. A week later, the shops
had no more plastic flags! He often ate fish fingers and salad |
in the cafeteria*, and followed this with chocolate [kæfə'tɪərɪə] ooOoo
ice cream. Suddenly these things became popular*. Some Ooo
girls brought a cassette recorder | and a camera to school,
to record* a dialogue* | with his voice | and make [rɪ'kɔ:d] – ['daɪəlɒg] Ooo
posters with the photos.

(100 words)

25. Im Deutschen und Englischen ähnliche Wörter; Homophone

Iris's dad found a good job in the West of England. He wanted to buy Iris | something new and quite expensive | for her birthday, because he knew | she was sad. He saw a skateboard. "But will she be able to ride it?" he wondered. "What if she falls off? Things with wheels can be dangerous. Perhaps I'll spend the money on a keyboard. She will be able to play beautiful music."

(72 words)

26. Fortsetzung von Diktat 25

In the end he spent a lot of money, and bought two presents: a keyboard and a white mouse | in a cage. He arrived at the house by car. When Iris's mum saw the mouse, her mouth dropped open. "We had mice before," she explained, "and they made too much work. Iris always had to find a classmate | to look after them | in the holidays. Don't you remember?"
But Iris was pleased* with the mouse. "It's all right," she [pli:zd]
whispered to her dad. "He's lovely. I'll write and tell you how he's doing."

(93 words)

27. Homophone

Form 9a is going on a school trip ˈ this week. In the classroom,
they're going through some rules. Mr Norton is saying:
"Walk on the pavement. If there isn't one, walk on the right
hand side ˈ of the road, so that you can see the traffic ˈ coming
towards* you. Take your swimming costume ˈ if you want to [təˈwɔːdz] oO
swim ˈ in the sea. But remember, I'm not a swimmer ˈ and I can't
rescue you. If anybody falls in, it's their problem, not mine.
(81 words)

28. Homophone; Fortsetzung von Diktat 27

Now, on these pieces of paper ˈ you will find a quiz ˈ about
the sights of the town. Write your name on your copy ˈ of
the quiz. Last year, one boy wrote a false* name ˈ on his quiz. [fɔːls]
Then he made it into a paper plane ˈ and threw it around the
bus. I hope nobody here ˈ will be so silly. If they are, their
parents will hear about it."
(68 words)

E Words in context 2

Während Mandy und Jane die Zeitschrift *Scrapbook* lesen, interessieren sich Toby und Daniel für die neueste Ausgabe von *Planet Earth*.

Holidays in Britain

1. **Ergänze den Text mit den vorgegebenen Wörtern. Als Hilfe sind die Betonungsmuster angegeben.**

• Welsh – Isles – fields – cows – crowds • harbours – peaceful – adverts – nature • UK – Skybus • escape – although – control – canals • lazily – passengers – difficult

• Two or three hundred years ago, most people stayed in and around one village all their lives. These days, it's different, as you can see from these Oo__________ for holidays in the OO_____________.

• Take a relaxing break in the Norfolk Broads. Sail Ooo_____________ along the Oo_____________ rivers and oO_____________. And don't worry if you've never tried to oO_______________ a boat before – it's not Ooo________________!

• Visit the Scilly O___________, a group of islands not far from Cornwall in the clear, blue Atlantic. Here you will find O___________ full of flowers in spring. oO_______________ one clearly can't drive to the islands, getting there isn't difficult. The 'OO_____________' flies to the Scilly Isles every day of the week from Bristol – Ooo_________________ are requested to check in an hour before the flight leaves – or you can travel by boat from Penzance.

• oO___________ from the O_______________ in the city, with a farm holiday in Wales. The kids will love watching the O____________ while they are being milked, and riding the ponies. Enjoy the O__________ coast line with its lovely Oo________________ full of colourful boats, or follow the Oo________________ trails in the forests and mountains of our national parks.

2. **Das Wort *lazily* ist ein Adverb. Wie schreibst du das Adjektiv?**

____

3. **In welchem Lernwort befindet sich ein stummes -s-?**

____

4. **Welche zwei Wörter haben die betonte Silbe [iː]?**

_____________ ________________

5. **Finde zwei Wörter mit dem Laut [aʊ], wie in *loud* und *mountain.***

______________ ______________

6. **Die Homophone *peace – piece***

a) After Alfie's birthday party, all the noisy children went home. His mother said '▼ at last! Now I can eat a ◇ of cake in ▼.'

Male die Zeichen: peace _____ piece _____

b) Füge jetzt die Wörter ein:

Jane is learning the cello, and she's practising a ____________ of music called 'The Swan' by Saint-Saëns. It's very _______ful. You can imagine the swan, sailing down the river in the ___________ and quiet of the evening. Jane plays other __________s, but this is her favourite.

7. **Die ähnlich klingenden Wörter *although – also***

a) Unterstreiche bei jedem Wort die betonte Silbe: although also

b) △ he's not very tall, Toby enjoys playing basketball. He ◆ plays tennis and football. Yesterday he and his friends played football at the park, △ it was raining.

Male die Zeichen: although _____ also _____

c) Füge ein:

___________ the Scilly Isles aren't far from the mainland, not many people go there. It isn't difficult to get there, ___________ it can be expensive. There are flights from Bristol, but there is _______a cheaper way to travel – by boat from Penzance.

8. Welche Art von Urlaub mögen die Briten am meisten?

	W	**H**	**B**	**L**	THEY
DI_FICULT	**H**	**O**	**R**	**I**	like
	A	**L**	**I**	**K**	
C_W	**T**	**I**	**T**	**E**	☐
HA_BOUR		**D**	**I**	**?**	☐
	S	**A**	**S**		
W_LSH	**O**	**Y**	**H**		☐
F_ELD	**R**	**S**			☐
	T		**P**		
ALTHOU_H		**D**	**E**		☐
PASSE_GERS	**O**	**O**	**O**		☐
	F		**P**		☐
			L		
			E		ones.

Holidays abroad

Many British people go abroad for their holidays. It's a small world!

9. Ergänze den Text mithilfe der angegebenen Buchstaben.

barbecues *Canyon* *choice* *especially* *experience* *grammar*
instruction *might* *neighbours* *Spanish* *wondering* *yourself*

Try a language holiday in Spain and learn **/Spnsh/**________________ within weeks. There is a **/chc/**______________ of different courses, with **/instrctn/**_______________ in vocabulary and **/grmmr/**______________ in the mornings, and afterwards trips, activities, parties and **/brbcs/** ________________. Don't miss this new **/exprnc/** __________________!

Bored with Europe? Want to see more of the world? America, the land of dreams, is only eight hours away. Visit the Grand **/Cnyn/**________________ and Salt Lake City. See the Arizona Desert for **/yrslf/**________________ – and lots more!

Are you **/wndrng/**__________________ where to spend your next holiday? You **/mght/**____________ like to try India for a change, **/espclly/**__________________ if you like Indian food or have **/nghbrs/**__________________ from India. We run cheap flights to Bombay – find out more by phoning us or visiting our website.

10. Drei Wörter haben den Laut [ʃ]. Welche?

________________ ________________ ________________

11. Revision: die fast-Homophone *spend – spent*

a) Form 9a ⌘ over twenty pounds on games for the classroom last week. Daniel says they mustn't ✻ any more. He says they've ⌘ enough for now.

Male die Zeichen: spend ____ spent _____

b) Bitte einsetzen:

They _________ a lot of money on board games, but they didn't _________ much on playing cards. Mandy asked: "How much did you _________ on board games? How much have you ___________ altogether?"

12. Revision: die fast-Homophone *we're – wear – where*

a) Do you know ◆ my best trousers are?
– Oh, you don't need them. ▼ going for a walk, not to a party. Anyway, It's very hot today. You could ▲ shorts.

Male die Zeichen: we're _____ wear _____ where _____

b) Am Telefon: Setze ein:

Hello, is that Pat? _________ are you?

– I'm in the car. Elaine is here, too. _________ on our way to John's party. I'm sure you could come, too.

– Oh, yes, I'd like to come. Shall I _________ a long skirt? Or is it a party _________ people _________ jeans?

13. Die Homophone *bored – board*

a) Daniel was often ▷ after school. One day he saw a notice on the notice ◁: Skate- ◁ club: meets at 4 p.m. every Wednesday at the gym. New members welcome.

Setze die Zeichen ein: board ____ bored ____

b) Jetzt kannst du die Wörter selber einfügen:

Are you sometimes _________? Look at the notice __________ at school or at your local sports centre. You'll find groups which play __________ games and card games like chess and bridge. Or if you want a more physical activity, try roller-blading or skate-_________ing.

14. Kannst du dieses SMS entschlüsseln?

R U going to B at the bar-B-Q ?

____?

A jungle in Britain

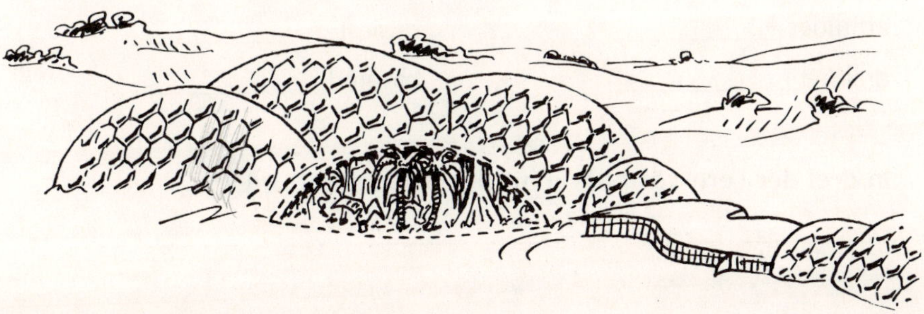

15. Ergänze den Text mithilfe der Lautschrift.

attitudes *bottom* *busiest* *covered* *drained* *expect*
industry *role* *since* *snow* *square* *success* *successful* *such*

If you want to experience a jungle but you don't want to go abroad, you should visit the biggest [sək'ses] ______________ story in Cornwall: the Eden Project, a large 'garden', including a 15,590 ['skweə] ____________ metre hothouse with plants [sʌtʃ] ___________ as rubber, rice and coffee. The building is ['kʌvəd] ______________ with plastic bubbles, and even if there is [snəʊ] ____________ outside, the air inside is warm and wet. Originally the site was a quarry *(Steinbruch)*, and a lot of water had to be [dreɪnd] _____________ out of the ['bɒtəm] _______________ of the quarry before building could begin. The Eden Project has been open [sɪns] ___________ the year 2001. So far, it has been very [sək'sesfl] _________________, and it's good for the tourist ['ɪndəstri] ____________ in Cornwall. The ticket manager, Christine Adie, joined the Eden Project in May 2000. She says: "Even on a quiet day we can [ɪk'spekt] __________________ about a thousand visitors, and on our ['bɪziəst] _______________ day we had about 4,500 visitors." One of the project's aims is to change people's ['ætɪtju:dz] _________________ to nature, and to help them to understand the [rəʊl] ________________ of plants in the environment.

16. Gib die Grundformen dieser Wörter an.

attitudes ____________ busiest _______________
drained ______________ covered _______________

17. In drei der Lernwörter kommt der Doppellaut [ks] vor:

__________________ __________________ ________________

18. Revision: die Homophone *its – it's*

a) The biology teacher is showing Form 9a a film about smoking. ◇ main message is that smoking is very bad for you. Lots of people think that ⌕ antisocial, too. ⌕ not very nice for people who don't smoke.

Trage die Zeichen ein: its ______ it's _____

b) Setze ein:

If you make a film about smoking, ________ message has to be very clear. Smoking is dangerous, and _______ always popular with younger people. That's because _______ something that only adults do; children aren't allowed to smoke.

19. Eine Pflanze, die im *Eden Project* gezüchtet wird, stellt die häufigste nicht-essbare Anbaupflanze der Welt dar. Der englische Name ist hier versteckt:

suc__essful

sn__w

expec__

at__itude

bott__m

si__ce

The Eden Project (continued)

20. Ergänze den Text mit den angegebenen Wörtern anhand der deutschen Übersetzung.

businesses *engineers* *exciting* *gifts* *marriage* *such* *support* *taste* *touch* *volunteers*

Groups of school children have guided tours where they can see, _________, smell and even _________ some of the plants. There is a shop where plants and __________ can be bought.

The project was started by Tim Smit together with a few _____________, but since then it has grown into a team of _______________ and scientists, and receives __________ from _______________ and councils. Tim Smit's right-hand man, Paul Travers, says that the project is _______________, but he feels drained because he works _________ long hours. He says it has had an effect on his _____________. His wife told him: Why don't you just take a sleeping bag to work?

Gruppen von Schulkindern bekommen Führungen, wo sie einige der Pflanzen sehen, berühren, riechen und sogar schmecken können. Es gibt einen Laden, wo Pflanzen und Geschenke gekauft werden können. Das Projekt wurde von Tim Smitt zusammen mit ein paar Freiwilligen begonnen, aber seitdem ist es zu einem Team aus Ingenieren und Wissenschaftlern angewachsen und bekommt Unterstutzung von Unternehmen und Gemeinden. Paul Travers, die rechte Hand Tim Smitts, meint, dass das Projekt spannend ist, aber er fühlt sich ausgelaugt, weil er solch einen langen Arbeitstag hat. Er sagt, es hat Auswirkung auf seine Ehe gehabt. Seine Frau sagte ihm: Warum nimmst du nicht einfach einen Schlafsack in die Arbeit mit?

21. Revision: die fast-Homophone *his – he's*

a) Dennis is an engineer. At the moment □ working on mobile phones, but ◆ real interest is computers.

Male die Zeichen: his ____ he's _____

b) Setze ein:

Dennis is at home. _________ packing _________ suitcase, because _________ company has sent him on a business trip. ________ coming back on Friday, in time for ________ daughter's birthday party.

22. Revision: die Homophone *hour – our; hours – ours*

a) When does ▼ train arrive in Paris? – At five past four. That's about an ▲ from now. The journey will take two and a half ▽. Where are ▼ bags? Are those ◇?

Trage die Zeichen ein: hour ___ our ___ hours ___ ours ___

b) Setze ein:

_________ dog has got a lot of energy. She can run around for half an _________ without stopping.

– Well, _________ is quite different. He lies in his basket for _________.

23. **Die fehlenden Buchstaben in diesen Sätzen ergeben den Namen einer Pflanze, die vom *Eden Project* gezüchtet wird. Kennst du sie? Bestimmt hast du sie schon mal gegessen!**

Long hours working on the __roject aren't good for Paul's marr__age.

You pay at the e__trance. Disabl__d people pay che__per rates.

The project is su__ported by businesses and councils.

The staff say they ex__ect about a thousand visitors a day.

The project was started by Tim Smitt and a few vo__unte__rs.

The name of this plant is: _ _ _ _ _ _ _ _ _ _ .

Marco Polo's journeys

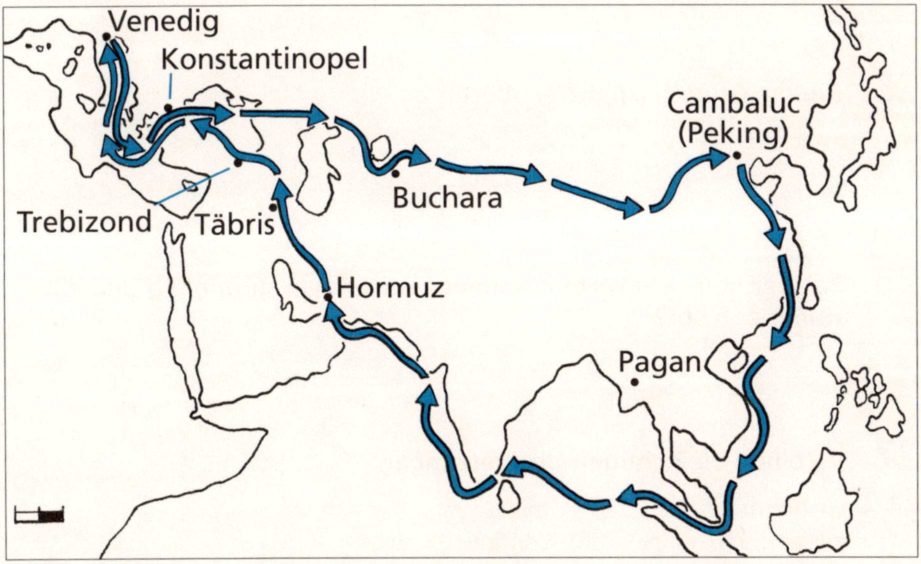

24. **Ergänze den Text mithilfe der vorgegebenen Wörter.**

attacked *business* *continue* *definitely* *enemies* *foreign* *mention* *robbed* *route* *spices* *thieves* *vehicles*

The Eden Project is **/dfntly/**____________ something which belongs to the 21st century with its modern technology; but **/frgn/**______________ travel is not new at all, as everybody knows. Take Marco Polo, for example. He was just 17 years old when he set off from Venice *(Venedig)* in the year 1271 with his father and uncle on a **/bsnss/**_______________trip to China, where they wanted to buy **/spcs/**_______________. There is no space here to **/mntn/**______________ all the places on their long **/rt/**_____________. They had no **/vhcls/**_____________, of course, and travelled on horseback. They had to make their way through sand storms and over snow-covered mountains. They were **/rbbd/**________________ by bands of **/thvs/** _________________. Sometimes people thought they were **/enms/** _______________, and **/attckd/**______________ them. Once, they became ill and could not **/cntn/**_______________ their journey for some months.

Tipp

Angegeben werden nur die Konsonanten der Wörter und die Anfangsvokale.

25. Gib die Grundform dieser Wörter an:

attacked__________	vehicles____________	robbed__________
spices____________	enemies___________	thieves__________

26. Bei welchen Lernwörtern kommen jeweils ein *stummes g* und ein *stummes h* vor?

_____________ _______________

27. Verbinde die richtigen Übersetzungen:

bestimmt	thief
ausländisch	continue
Gewürze	definitely
Dieb	foreign
fortsetzen	spices

28. Revision: die Homophone *there – their – they're*

a) Mandy, Jane and Daniel are doing a project about smoking. ✻ interviewing ◆ families and neighbours about ◆ opinions on smoking. They've already found out that ▲ are lots of different opinions.

Male die Zeichen: there _____ their _____ they're ______

b) Setze ein:

Jane and Mandy live in the same road, and Mr and Mrs Wheeler are ______ neighbours. __________ quite old. They've got a small house, and they've lived _______ ever since _________ first child was born. ________ not smokers, but __________ grown-up son smokes.

29. Die Homophone *knows* – *nose*

a) Everybody ▲ that Pinocchio had a long ◆, but not everybody ▲ why. His ◆ grew long because he didn't tell the truth.

Trage die Zeichen ein: knows _____ nose _____

b) Setze ein:

There's something wrong with Vanda's _________. She's been to the ear, ______ and throat specialist, and she _________ that she will have to have an operation. She isn't looking forward to it, but she _________ it's the best thing to do. Afterwards, her ________ will be fine again.

30. Doppel- oder Einzelkonsonant? Die Lösungsbuchstaben ergeben den Namen einer Stadt, die auf der Route Marco Polos lag.

		Doppelkons.	Einzelkons.
a__ack	t(t)	H	K
de__initely	f(f)	A	O
conti__ue	n(n)	N	R
fo__eign	r(r)	T	M
busine__	s(s)	U	O
e__emy	n(n)	N	Z

Marco Polo and his two relatives passed through __ __ __ __ __ __ on their way to China.

Marco Polo's journeys (continued)

31. **Ergänze die Fortsetzung der Geschichte mithilfe der Übersetzung.**

belonged *caught* *celebrations* *Chinese* *died* *famous*
fortunately *journeys* *palace* *prison* *spoons* *while*

__________, none of them __________, and four years after they started, the three men reached the east coast of China. They stayed in a __________ which __________ to Kublai Khan, a very rich __________ emperor. There were fantastic __________ with golden cups and __________. Marco Polo loved China, and lived there for seventeen years. Later, he returned to Venice and took part in a sea battle. He was __________ by the enemy and was put into __________. __________ he was there, he dictated the story of his __________ through Asia to another prisoner, and so Marco Polo and his story became __________.

Glücklicherweise starb keiner und vier Jahre nachdem sie aufgebrochen waren, erreichten die drei Männer die Ostküste Chinas. Sie wohnten in einem Palast, der Kublai Khan gehörte, einem sehr reichen chinesischen Kaiser. Es gab fantastische Feiern, mit goldenen Tassen und Löffeln. Marco Polo liebte China und er lebte dort siebzehn Jahre. Später kehrte er nach Venedig zurück und nahm an einer Seeschlacht teil. Er wurde von dem Feind gefangen und ins Gefängnis gesperrt. Während er dort war, diktierte er die Geschichte seiner Reisen durch Asien einem anderen Häftling und so wurden Marco Polo und seine Geschichte berühmt.

32. **Gib die Grundformen von *caught* und *died* an:**

__________ __________

33. **Zwei der Lernwörter enden mit unbetontem [əs]. Welche?**

__________ __________

34. **Ergänze:**

cel__bration pris__n fort__n__t__ly journ__s __hinese

35. Revision: die Homophone *by – buy*

a) If we go ▶ train, we'll be there ▶ ten o'clock. Let's ◆ a ticket now!

Male die Zeichen: by ______ buy ______

b) Setze ein:

Fabian is going to ________ the latest book ________ J.K. Rowlings. There's a bookshop ______ the station. It closes at six o'clock, so he must be there ______ five to six at the latest.

A journey to the stars

36. Ergänze den Text mithilfe der Betonungsmuster.

Die Wörter, nach der Zahl der Silben geordnet:

edge *death* *secret* *argued* *believed* *Christian* *alive*
similar *arguments* *disagreed* *executed*

Thousands of years ago, people oO__________________ that if you made a very long journey, you might fall straight off the O__________ of the earth. They also believed that the sun went round the earth. Copernicus realized that the earth went round the sun, but not everybody agreed with him, and there were many Ooo________________. He wrote a book, and it was published *(veröffentlicht)* on the day of his O__________ in 1543. Galileo, another early scientist, had Ooo_________________ ideas. The Church Oo_______________ that these ideas went against the Oo_______________ religion, and Galileo received a Oo_______________ message which told him to keep quiet. He didn't, and he was made a prisoner in his own house. He was lucky to be oO________________. In those days, people who ooO__________________ openly with the church could be Oooo______________________.

37. Schreibe die Grundform zu diesen Wörtern.

argued ____________ executed ______________

disagreed ____________ believed _____________

38. **Wann ist Kopernikus gestorben? Unterstreiche die richtige Jahresangabe.**

a) fifteen hundred forty-three

b) fifteen hundred and forty-three

c) fifteen forty-three

39. **Für welche Wörter aus Übung 36 stehen hier die deutschen Ausdrücke?**

a) Rand ________________

b) am Leben ________________

c) geheim ________________

d) ähnlich ____________________

40. **Die ähnlich klingenden Wörter *of – off***

a) The plane takes ▷ in three quarters ▽ an hour. Let me take a photo ▽ you before you leave. You'll have to take that hat ▷, ▽ course; it hides the top half ▽ your face.

Trage die Zeichen ein: of _____ off ______

b) Setze die Wörter ein:

Tony's terrible. He often forgets to turn _____ the light when he goes out _____ a room. He leaves his clothes where he takes them _____ - usually in the middle ______ the bathroom floor. Lots _____ children ______ his age are the same, but not all _____ them.

41. **Wo wurde Kopernikus geboren? Die fehlenden Buchstaben hier ergeben die Antwort.**

cu__board r__und wa__k thous__nd agai__st __isagree

___ ___ ___ ___ ___ ___

A new age

42. **Ergänze den Text mithilfe der Lautschrift.**

cable *catalogues* *chess* *communication* *contact* *control* *education* *heart* *mysteries* *news* *surgeon* *surgery* *techniques*

Now, in the 21st century, most of the world's ['mɪstərɪz] ________________ have been cleared up. [edʒu'keɪʃn] ____________________ has improved, and there are schools for everybody. With telephones and e-mail, [kəmju:nɪ'keɪʃn] ____________________ has become easier. Through the Internet you can find out the latest [nju:z] __________, find information, order things from mail order ['kætəlɒgz] ________________ and ['kɒntækt] ______________ people with the same interests or problems. You can even play a game of [tʃes] __________ or pool with somebody you will never meet. You can watch programmes from other countries on ['keɪbl] _____________ TV. New [tek'ni:ks] ______________________ in ['sɜ:dʒərɪ] ______________ mean that a ['sɜ:dʒən] _________________ can [kən'trəʊl] _______________ an operation on a [hɑ:t] _____________, for example, by computer. We live in a new age – the Information Age.

43. **Diese Wörter werden alle mit *-ea-* geschrieben. In einem Wort wird es anders als in den übrigen ausgesprochen. In welchem?**

head *healthy* *heart* *death* *dead*

44. **Schreibe den Singular:**

catalogues	techniques	mysteries
__________	__________	__________

45. Die Homophone *through* – *threw*

a) Fabian got into trouble when he ▽ a ball ▼ a window.

Trage die Zeichen ein: through ____ threw _____

b) Ergänze:

Fabian's dad was looking for an important letter. He looked ____________ everything on his desk. 'Oh, dear,' said his wife. 'Perhaps I __________ it away.'

46. Die Nachrichtenübermittlung hat sich in den letzten 200 Jahren erheblich verbessert. Rate mal, wie man diesen Satz ergänzen müsste, damit er stimmt:

In 1805, Nelson won the Battle of Trafalgar. It took two and a half ____________ for the news to reach London.

(hours? days? oder etwas anderes?)

Die Lösung findest du, wenn du die fehlenden Buchstaben in den Sätzen unten in bestehender Reihenfolge zusammenschreibst.

When Daniel and Andy __rite l__tters to th__ir Grandma, they __now that __he will write back.

A holiday on the moon

47. Ergänze den Text mithilfe der Symbole.

✻ requests – communications
▼ coins – differences
▽ experience – purses
◆ moon – survey
▲ spare – space
❁ unless – really

With better ✻ ____________________, people are beginning to think that they've seen everything. They want a new ▽ _________________ – a holiday with a difference. Germans who go on holiday to Italy find fewer and fewer ▼ __________________. Even the ▼ _______________ in their ▽ _________________ are the same as at home. So what about a holiday on the ◆ ________________ this year?
Well, you might laugh, but a ◆ _________________ has shown that forty-three percent (43%) of all Germans would like to be astronauts and travel in ▲ _______________, and several travel agents have had ✻ ____________________ for holidays on the moon. One day it will ❁ ___________ happen, but it will be very expensive. People won't be able to take a holiday in space ❁ ____________ they have some ▲ _______________ money in the bank – about twenty-five million euros.

48. Schreibe den Singular hin:

differences ____________ purses _____________

49. Welche Wörter aus Übung 47 (in der Grundform) entsprechen diesen deutschen Begriffen?

a) übrig____________ b) Bitte______________

c) Umfrage____________ d) Erlebnis________________

50. Revision: Halte auseinander: *how – who*

a) Hier sind zwei deutsche Wörter, die sich auf *how* bzw. *who* reimen. Schreibe sie neben das entsprechende Wort.

blau ________ du __________

b) We would like to go away on holiday, but there's a problem. ▷ will look after our cat while we're away? And ◀ will the cat get in and out of the house?

Trage die Zeichen ein: how _____ who _____

c) Setze ein:

Fabian, a boy _______ comes from Germany, is going to Karlsruhe for two weeks. Jane asks him:

_______ are you going to stay with? ______ long are you going to stay there? _______ will you travel?

51. **Wie hieß der erste Mensch im All? Sein Name versteckt sich in den Anfangsbuchstaben jedes <u>zweiten</u> Wortes in dieser Kette.**

C A B L E G U I T A R B R A I N A R R O W E X E C U T E G R A F F I T I C H E S S
A S T R O N A U T C E L E B R A T E R E Q U E S T O P E R A T E I N D U S T R Y
U N L E S S N E W S

Tipp

Fange mit dem zweiten Wort an.

The class representative

52. **Setze die Wörter passend in den Text ein. Als Hilfe sind die Konsonanten der gesuchten Wörter angegeben.**

choose *graffiti* *hurt* *messages* *nationalities* *opinions*
people *politely* *popular* *properly* *term* *voted* *worry*

These days, **/ppl/**______________ of different **/ntnlts/**_________________ understand each other better. But you still sometimes see **/grfft/**_________________ on the wall, telling blacks and others to 'go home'. Anonymous **/mssgs/**______________________ like that can **/hrt/**__________. Some black kids don't **/wrry/**______________ – like Ben, for example. He's a **/pplr/**_________________ boy at school, and when it was time to **/chs/**________________ the class representative last **/trm/**_____________, most of the class **/vtd/**_______________ for him. He wants to do the job **/prprly/**_______________, and if there are any problems or requests, Ben goes to the teacher and **/pltly/**_______________ and clearly explains the pupils' **/opnns/**_______________ to her.

53. Eines der Lernwörter steht im *simple past*. Wie sieht die Grundform aus?

____

54. Wie lautet der Singular von *nationalities*? ______________________

55. Die ähnlich klingenden Wörter *this* – *these*

a) Schreibe die sich reimenden Wörter nebeneinander.

keys ___________ kiss ___________

b) Verbinde:

this
these

easy questions
trousers
sweatshirt
shoes
farmer
people
funny mice
address
detective
money
bag of sweets

c) What are you going to wear at the school disco, Toby?
– I think I'll wear □ jeans and ◇ white shirt. Oh and □ black shoes.

Trage die Zeichen ein: this ____ these ____

d) Setze ein:

Mother: Are you still awake at _______ time? You go to bed very late _______ days. What's _______? A book of horror stories! You shouldn't read _________ frightening books late at night.

56. **Ben möchte eine bestimmte Sportart ausprobieren. Kannst du herausfinden, woran er dabei denkt?**

__orry

ne__ghbour

opinio__

__ifficult

choo__e

h__rt

prope__ly

graf__iti;

espec__ally

autum__

forei__n

The problem page

57. **Ergänze den Text.**

since *fat* *hates* *real* *mirrors* *perfumes* *mostly* *themselves* *including* *barbecue* *anyway* *miserable* *celebrating*

Tipp Die Wörter sind nach den Betonungsmustern geordnet.

Linda: I'm so Ooo__________. I'm sure that everybody in my class O_________ me. I have no O_________ friends, and I haven't been invited to any parties O__________ I was about five – until now. Joanna, a classmate of mine, lives on a large farm, and she's Oooo_______________ her 13th birthday with a Ooo_______________. She has invited the whole class, oOo________________ me. They're Oo___________ boys. What shall I do? All the other girls spend the break time putting make-up on with little Oo__________, and making oO_____________ smell nice with different Oo___________. I don't know anything about make-up. Ooo__________, I'm O________ and not at all beautiful. I know I won't enjoy the barbecue.

58. **Unterstreiche in der Wortauswahl von Übung 57 den betonten Laut [e] (wie in *pet*, *head*). Er kommt dreimal vor.**

59. **In welchen zwei Wörtern kommt der Laut [juː] (wie in *you*, *uniform*) vor?**

______________________ ______________________

60. **Wie lauten die Grundformen dieser Wörter?**

hates ____________ perfumes ________________

including ________________ celebrating ____________

61. **Revision: die Homophone *know* – *no***

a) There's a notice at Campbell Camping Site. It says: ◁ dogs allowed. Luckily Sue and Terry ▷ another camping site near there, where dogs are allowed, so that's ◁ problem.

Trage die Zeichen ein: know ______ no ______

b) Setze ein:

Do you __________ if the supermarket is still open? There's ________ milk in the fridge.

– Oh dear. ______, it isn't open. But I ___________ a little Indian shop which is usually open until ten.

62. **Was für ein Mädchen ist Joanna? Du kannst etwas über sie erfahren, wenn du die deutschen und englischen Begriffe miteinander verbindest.**

feiern barb__cue

echt __elebrate

elend themsel__es

sie sich mi__ror

Grillfest mis__rable

Spiegel rea__

Joanna is a __ __ __ __ __ __ girl.

Tipp

Die in den englischen Wörtern fehlenden Buchstaben sortierst du nach der Reihenfolge der deutschen Wörter, dann findest du das Lösungswort leicht.

Some good ideas for Linda

63. Ergänze den Text mithilfe der Symbole.

⌘ poems – sugar	◆ fridge – operate	▼ guitar – mood
▲ tears – success	⁎ arrows – coal	○ oven – plug
❁ cheer – positive		

Margaret: Poor you! You are your own worst enemy. Dry your ▲ ____________ and try to take a more ❁ ______________ attitude to life. If you're in a bad ▼ ______________, nobody will want to talk to you. So ❁ ____________ up and find a role for yourself. Perhaps you play the ▼ ______________ – if so, take that along to the party. Live music is always popular. Or you can ○ ___________ in the CD player and ◆ __________________ it, or put ⁎ _____________ on the fire, bring food from the ◆ __________________, get baked potatoes out of the ○ ____________ and carry ⌘ __________________, salt and pepper to the tables. Help Joanna to make signs with ⁎ ______________ to show where things are. If you're good at writing ⌘ _______________, see if you can write one about Joanna and read it out at the barbecue. Think about others – that's the secret of ▲ _____________. Good luck!

64. Zwei Lernwörter beginnen mit dem Buchstaben o. Ordne sie den Lauten zu.

[ɒ] (wie in *got*)______________ [ʌ] (wie in *bus*)________________

65. Finde Lernwörter, die sich in der Grundform mit diesen Wörtern reimen:

dear _________ you'd __________ role _____________

66. Revision: die Homophone *see* – *sea*

a) Can you ▼ that island in the ▲?

see ______ sea ______

b) Setze ein:

When you ________ postcards, you think the _______ must always be blue. You only _______ the real colour when you go to the coast and ________ it with your own eyes. The _________ is usually green, or even brown.

67. Möchtest du wissen, wie es Linda bei dem Grillfest erging? Die richtigen fehlenden Buchstaben geben dir Auskunft. Ein ○ steht für „kein Buchstabe".

positiv__	e: Linda was miserable	○: Linda had a great time
po__m	e: at first	i: all evening
g__itar	○: and played	u: but cheered up when she played
__ven	o: a miming game	u: solitaire
sug__r	a: with the others.	e: in a corner.
ar__ow	○: Later she talked	r: Later she danced
fri__e	dg: with Peter	g: to Joanna
su__ess	c: and decided	cc: and knew
m__d	u: she should go home.	oo: she was happy.

Auch die falschen Antworten ergeben eine witzige Alternative.

Tipp

F Word workshop 2

1. Plural-s; 3. Person Singular-s

1. **Unterstreiche die Grundform.**

Beispiel: watches

a) crisps b) churches c) lakes d) moves e) agrees
f) classes g) matches h) dialogues

2. **Schreibe die Grundform hin:**

a) dictionaries *dictionary* b) factories __________
c) carries __________ d) journeys __________
e) wives __________ f) shelves __________

3. **Wenn das Wort in Klammern stimmt, hake es ab. Falls nicht, schreibe die richtige Form in die Lücke.**

a) A **(car)** ✓ is a four-wheeled **(vehicle)** __________ designed to carry about five people.

b) Two hundred **(year)** *years* ago there were no **(car)** __________, only horse-drawn **(vehicle)** __________.

c) Do you believe in **(fairy)** __________? Jasmin **(believe)** __________ in them, but her **(brother)** __________ don't.

d) The **(park)** __________ near her house has lots of **(tree)** __________ and **(path)** __________. She has found a **(place)** __________ where she's sure a **(fairy)** __________ **(live)** __________.

e) If anyone **(touch)** __________ Andy's hamster, it **(run)** __________ away. But it doesn't **(run)** __________ away if Andy **(touch)** __________ it. Do you keep **(hamster)** __________?

f) When Fabian's dad got back from a **(business)** __________ trip, he found six **(fax)** __________ and twenty e-mails waiting for him.

Du solltest sieben Häkchen gesetzt haben.

Tipp

4. Finde auch hier heraus, welche Form schon stimmt, und welche du erst noch verändern musst.

a) The **(busker)** ______________ in the underground usually play nice **(music)** ____________.

b) Fabian always **(hurry)** ______________ to **(catch)** ______________ the bus in the morning. Paul doesn't **(hurry)** ______________; he usually gets up and **(go)** __________ out of the house early.

c) Lots of **(business)** ______________ and art **(gallery)** ____________ produce **(catalogue)** ______________ of their wares.

d) In Britain the **(railway)** ________________ are being repaired, so the **(train)** ________________ are often delayed, and people on long **(journey)** ______________ can **(expect)** __________________ to **(arrive)** _____________ between one and two **(hour)** ____________ late.

e) Although the **(train)** ________________ are often late, the **(bus)** ______________ usually run on time.

f) In English, you usually **(start)** ____________ a speech with the words: **(Lady)** ______________ and gentlemen …

Hier solltest du sechs Häkchen gesetzt haben.

Tipp

5. Auch hier kannst du das Plural-s und die 3. Person Singular üben.

a) **(Life)** ______ in the country is healthier than **(life)** _________ in a big **(city)** _______.

b) Jane is reading a book about the **(life)** _____________ of the great **(composer)** ______________________; Beethoven and Mozart, for example.

c) The **(police)** ______________ have posters around the town, saying: 'Look out, there's a **(thief)** _______________ about!'

d) There really are a lot of **(thief)** ____________ who **(climb)** __________ in through **(window)** ____________ and take expensive **(jewellery)** _________ and other **(thing)** ____________.

e) Aunt Millie always puts jam on the table at tea-time. If there are **(visitor)** ____________ there, they often ask: 'Did you make it **(yourself)** ____________?'

f) Daniel and Paul's mum and dad are going out. They tell the boys: 'You'll have to look after **(yourself)** __________ this evening.'

Tipp Du solltest acht Häkchen gesetzt haben.

2. *Simple past* und *past participle*

6. Unterstreiche die Grundformen.

controlled	celebrated	drained	argued	attacked
panicked				
plugged	pushed	robbed	chased	
pulled	added	visited	travelled	

7. Diese *simple-past*-Formen sind sich ähnlich. Schreib die Grundform hin und kreise das Wort ein, das sich von den beiden anderen unterscheidet.

cried________ died ________ tried____________

8. Passiv-Formen. Ergänze die Sätze mit dem passenden Verb im Passiv. Du kannst selber entscheiden, welches Verb jeweils sinnvoll ist. Ein Wort passt nirgendwohin. Kreise es ein.

kill	*visit*	*scan*	*chase*	*support*	*shock*
die	*attack*	~~*count*~~	*plug*	*celebrate*	*rob*

a) After the summer bazaar, the money was *counted*. It came to four hundred pounds.

b) Help! Stop that thief! I've been ______________.

c) Yesterday, Sarah's rabbit was ______________ by a dog. Luckily, it managed to get away.

d) The Eden Project is ______________ by businesses and community councils.

e) The Eden Project is ______________ by all sorts of people, including tourists and classes of schoolchildren.

f) The Queen Mother's 100th birthday was ______________ in July 2000, although she wasn't actually 100 until 4th August.

g) When Princess Diana was ______________ in a car crash in 1997, the whole British nation was very ______________.

h) Has the CD player been ______________ in yet? I'd like to use it.

i) Has that photo been ______________ into your dad's computer yet?

9. **Unregelmäßige Verben.** Diese Sätze haben je zwei Lücken; in eine gehört die Grundform des Verbs (in Klammern angedeutet), in die andere das *simple past* bzw. *past participle*.

a) Why do I __________ things so often? I've __________ my keys now. **(l-s-)**

b) Can you __________ my keys for me? You __________ my watch yesterday. **(f-nd)**

c) A new school is being __________ near the church. I don't know why they have to __________ another one – there are enough already. **(buil-)**

d) I don't think that explanation was ________________ by everybody. Did you ________________ it? **(underst- -d)**

e) Do you _________ Asterix comics? I've never ___________ one in my life. **(r- -d)**

f) The next Stamp Club meeting is being ___________ in the library. We can't ___________ it in Room 118 this week. **(h-ld)**

3. -ing-Formen

10. **Unterstreiche die Gerund-Formen und schreibe ihre Grundformen auf die Schreibzeilen.**

<u>Ice-skating</u> is fun. The important thing about learning to skate is practising how to stop. Stopping is difficult if you haven't done it before. And falling over can be painful. Skiing is another popular winter sport, but getting to the mountains can be difficult, and driving on icy roads is no fun at all. Avalanches *(Lawinen)* are a danger in the mountains. Don't go off the piste – just imagine lying in the snow for hours and having to be rescued. Imagine trying to get out, and finding that you're trapped.

ice-skate, ____

____

____

11. Kennst du das Märchen *Goldilocks and the three bears*? Ein kleines Mädchen geht in ein Haus, wo Mummy, Daddy und Baby Bear wohnen. Sie probiert den Haferbrei, die Stühle und die Betten. Als die drei Bären von einem Spaziergang zurückkehren, sind sie entsetzt.

In the kitchen:

Daddy Bear: Somebody has been tasting my porridge!

Mummy Bear: Somebody has been tasting my porridge, too!

Baby Bear: Somebody has been tasting my porridge, and has eaten it all up!

In the living room:

Daddy Bear: Somebody has been sitting in my chair!

Mummy Bear: Somebody has been sitting in my chair, too!

Baby Bear: Somebody has been sitting in my chair, and has broken it all to pieces!

Upstairs:

Daddy Bear: Somebody has been lying in my bed!

Mummy Bear: Somebody has been lying in my bed, too!

Baby Bear: Somebody has been lying in my bed, and there she is! Look, she has just woken up.

Finde die Hauptverben in jedem Teil und schreibe sie in der Grundform hin.

In the kitchen: *taste* ______________ ______________

In the living room: ______________ ______________

Upstairs: ______________ ______________

12. **Was fehlt in diesen *-ing*-Formen noch? Suche die richtige Alternative aus und erfahre, was Goldilocks noch passiert ist.**

d__ing	**ie:**	Goldilocks wasn't frightened when she saw the bears.
	y:	Goldilocks was very frightened when she saw the bears.
arg__ing	**u:**	She got up and ran to the window,
	ue:	She got out of bed and ran to the bedroom door,
ro__ing	**bb:**	and escaped.
	b:	and then she ran into the kitchen.
contro__ing	**ll:**	In the end, she managed to find her way home,
	l:	She managed to hide under the table for a short while,
cove__ing	**rr:**	but the bears found her there.
	r:	and the bears made some more porridge.
disagr__ing	**e:**	Goldilocks was never seen again.
	ee:	Goldilocks was never allowed to go into the forest alone again.

13. **Hier sind einige Verben in der Grundform. Schreibe ihre *-ing*-Formen hin:**

a) arrange__________ b) carry__________ c) tie__________

d) escape__________ e) fix__________ f) offer__________

g) travel__________ h) panic__________ i) plug__________

j) scan__________ k) snow__________

4. Steigerung der Adjektive und Adverbien

14. **Ergänze die Grundformen der Adjektive. Du findest die gesuchten Wörter im jeweiligen Satz.**

Beispiel: Mandy was looking for a *cheap* pair of ice skates, so Iris told her which shop had the cheapest skates.

a) Mr Norton often tells Form 9a that they're too __________. He says they're the noisiest class in the school.

b) Lady, the dog that belongs to Fabian's family, is getting fatter and fatter. They have no idea why she is so _______.

c) Fabian's little sister, Jasmin, is quite _________ for her age, but her friend Lucy is even smaller.

d) The pavements in Wolstanton town centre aren't _________ enough, so they're being made wider.

15. Füge jetzt Formen mit *-er* bzw. *-est* in die Lücken ein.

a) Daniel hasn't got a very good opinion of Robert. 'He's crazy,' he says. 'Even __________ than he was last year.'

b) You might think that Daniel is the __________ person in his family. On Saturdays, he stays in bed until eleven o'clock. But he's not really lazy. He's growing, so he needs more sleep.

c) Mrs Hollywood is one of the ___________ teachers at the Wolstanton High School. But although she's strict, she's always kind to people in trouble.

d) There's a strong smell in the Browns' house, and it's ________________ of all near the cat's basket.

e) Strange things happen at the old castle. The _____________ thing of all is the ghost that disappears through the wall.

f) Iris has gone to France again on a Guide camp. Her mum is glad that she has arrived safely, but she'll be even ___________ when Iris comes home again.

g) Alfie wants to know who is the ____________ person in the world. His parents think it might be Bill Gates – he's a very rich man.

h) Fabian's mum and dad are German. They think English people are ______________ than Germans, because they often say 'please' and 'thank you'. Actually, Germans are polite too, but in different ways.

16. Gib die Grundformen dieser Adverbien an:

a) luckily________ b) really________

c) suddenly__________ d) wonderfully _____________

17. Auch hier werden die Grundformen gesucht:

a) terribly__________ b) expensively____________

c) horribly______________ d) finely_________

e) Alle diese Grundformen enden mit dem Buchstaben _____.

f) Streiche durch, was nicht stimmt:
Bei Adjektiven, die mit *-able* / *-ible* enden, wird bei der Bildung des Adverbs das End-e **beibehalten / weggelassen.** Das „*l*" der Grundform **bleibt als Einzelkonsonant / wird verdoppelt**.

g) Wie lautet das Adverb von *miserable*? ____________________

18. Ergänze die angefangenen Wörter zu Adverbien anhand der deutschen Entsprechungen:

faul	l_____
bestimmt	defini______
besonders	especial_____
wirklich	re____
glücklicherweise	fortu_____
genau	exac____
geduldig	pat_____
erfolgreich	succes____

Der erste Buchstabe in jedem Wort, den du selber hinzugefügt hast, ergibt den Namen einer Insel, von der du schon gehört hast, wo du aber bestimmt noch nie gewesen bist: ____________________.

5. Apostrophe und Groß- und Kleinschreibung

19. Bei jedem dieser Paare ist nur ein Apostroph möglich. Weißt du wo?

thiefs	stairs
count	cant
ladys	sandals
wont	want
theirs	theres

Tipp

Erinnerst du dich noch? Den Genitiv mit *-s* verwendest du meist nur bei Personen und Tieren.

20. Finde in jeder Zeile den Begriff, der hinsichtlich der Groß- und Kleinschreibung aus der Reihe tanzt (d. h. er wird als einziger groß- bzw. kleingeschrieben).

SISTER	BROTHER	KAREN	COUSIN
VILLAGE	LONDON	TOWN	CITY
CHRISTIAN	QUIET	RELIGIOUS	GOOD
LAND	COUNTRY	PLACE	ITALY
MODERN	RICH	STRANGE	AMERICAN
ETC.	TV	OK	CD
BIOLOGY	MATHS	SKIING	GEOGRAPHY
CHRISTMAS	WINTER	BOXING DAY	EASTER
MONDAY	TODAY	FRIDAY	TUESDAY

21. Caroline und ihr Bruder Stephen sind mit ihren Eltern nach Essex gezogen. Mandy hat eine E-Mail von Caroline bekommen, wobei Caroline einige Großbuchstaben und Apostrophe vergessen hat. Kreise die Stellen ein, wo ein Großbuchstabe fehlt. Verwende für die fehlenden Apostrophe einen Farbstift.

Hi Mandy!

How are you? Weve moved in and of course I can't find anything. Everything is in boxes. Yesterday I had to buy a new pair of boots because my old

ones are in a box – nobody knows which one. We had to borrow some dishes from the neighbours, mr and Mrs stone, because ours have disappeared. My mother keeps telling us not to break the neighbours dishes – she's getting on my nerves a bit and I think were getting on hers. My bike arrived without its basket. I don't know where it is, its not in the garage or in the house. I'm borrowing Stephens for now, but he doesn't know. I'm sure he wont want me to have it when he knows. How is school these days? Ours is quite nice, its a bit old but most of the teachers are friendly, especially mrs Brice. She takes us for maths and Physics. She comes from wolstanton, and her aunt lives in Boulton street, the same street as my grandmother! I've got a new friend, an indian girl called Samantha Patel. Her parents gave her an english name so that she wouldn't feel different. They don't celebrate christian festivals as theyre hindus, and her dad usually works on christmas day. He's a bus driver, and he works for a london bus company called cheetah transport.
My new address is: 15, Oak tree Road, Stock, Essex. Youve got my e-mail address anyway and Ive got yours.
Love, Caroline.

Tipp

Die Zahl der fehlenden Großbuchstaben ist durch 4 teilbar. Diese Zahl ist um 6 größer als die Zahl der fehlenden Apostrophe. Vergleiche deine Ergebnisse mit den Lösungen im hinteren Teil des Buches.

6. Zusammen- und Getrenntschreibung

22. Ein Wort oder zwei? Finde die zwei Lösungswörter, indem du danach sortierst, ob es sich um ein Wort oder zwei Wörter handelt.

micro	phone	K
door	bell	E
musical	instrument	F
centi	metre	T
grammar	exercise	R
grand	parents	T
tourist	industry	E
al	though	L
all	right	N
vegetable	curry	C
rail	way	E
special	offer	H
our	selves	D
him	self	R
escape	route	H
home	less	U
pocket	money	O
rock	band	R
any	way	M
cable	television	N

One word: _ _ _ _ _ _ _ _ _ _ _

Two words: _ _ _ _ _ _   _ _ _ _

7. Verschiedene Buchstaben- und Lautkombinationen

23. Doppel- oder Einzelkonsonant?
Diese Schilder sind beschädigt. Vervollständige sie mit Einzel- oder Doppelkonsonanten. Füge die Konsonanten, die übrig bleiben, in die Lösungszeile, um das Wort für ein „natürliches" Getränk zu bekommen.

l l c m m l k r l m l s

1. National Ga___ery
2. Fo___eign Office
3. Government Co___unication Headquarters
4. Publi___ Library
5. Buckingham Pa___ace
6. Passport Contro___
7. Strangeways Pri___on

Lösungszeile: ____i_______________

24. Ergänze die Definitionen. Es geht um Einzel- und Doppelkonsonanten.

a) Two groups of people who attack each other are en______ies.
b) A helper who doesn't get paid is a vol______eer.
c) A gui___ is an instrument with six strings.
d) The bot______ of a hill is the lowest point of the hill.
e) A ro__e is the function of a person within a team or in a play.

Einige der folgenden Buchstaben brauchst du.

a a e l m m m n n o r t t t t u u u

Übrig bleibt eine englische Jahreszeit: ________________

25. **Ergänze die angegebenen Wörter mithilfe der Lautschrift. Wer hat das traditionelle Fußballspiel (Lehrer gegen Schüler) an der *Wolstanton High School* dieses Jahr gewonnen? Das Lösungswort verrät es dir.**

[sə'pɔ:t] – ['ætɪtju:d] – [sə'pəʊzd] – [grə'fi:ti] – ['dɪfrənt] – ['pæsɪndʒə]

				s	u	p	__	__	__	t	
		a	t	t	i	t	__	d	e		
				s	u	p	__	__	__	e	d
		g	r	a	f	__	__	__	i		
d	i	f	__	__	c	__	__	t			
				p	a	s	__	__	__	g	er

The ___ ___ ___ ___ ___ ___ won.

26. **Unterstreiche die stummen Konsonanten.**

A lot of people leave the British Isles in summer and early autumn for a holiday abroad, although most of them don't speak a foreign language. They give their key to a neighbour, park their vehicle at the airport and set off into the unknown.

27. **Der Laut [ɪ]**
Setze ein:

i *y* *u* *ui* *i* *i* *y* *i* *i* *i* *i* *i* *ui* *i* *i* *u*

Was bleibt übrig?

g__tar	fr__dge	b__sc__t	m__stery	s__nce
rel__gion	str__ct	s__mbol	r__ch	b__sy
d__sagree	b__siness	s__milar	m__serable	

28. **In jeder Zeile sind drei Wörter; zwei mit dem Laut [aɪ] und eins mit dem Laut [i:]. Unterstreiche in jeder Zeile das Wort mit [i:] und finde die Antwort auf diese Frage: Welches Land der Welt produziert den meisten Tabak?**

a)	N: alive	S: directions	C: graffiti
b)	H: field	P: Chinese	E: smile
c)	A: polite	I: police	P: die

d) A: biology	I: spice	N: technique
e) N: title	L: hide	A: vehicle

Lösung: ______________________

29. Bis auf zwei Wörter haben alle diese Wörter eine bestimmte Laut-Kombination gemeinsam. Klammere die zwei Ausnahmen ein.

argue – barbecue – beautiful – communication – continue – execution – few – Hindu – menu – perfume – stupid - tube – tune – UK – uniform – useful – Urdu – youth

30. Welches Tier ist am längsten trächtig (20 Monate)? Ein Wortpaar reimt sich nicht (es geht nur um die Endsilben). Die Antwort steht bei diesem Paar.

a) astronaut – short	blue whale
b) bought – pilot	Asian elephant
c) report – caught	African elephant
d) support – taught	Indian rhinoceros

31. Ähnlichkeiten zwischen deutschen und englischen Wörtern.

Bei diesen deutschen Wörtern musst du nur ein -e streichen oder hinzufügen, um das entsprechende englische Wort zu bekommen. Manchmal musst du sogar nichts verändern.

ASTRONAUT	ATTACKE	LEGENDE	ROUTE
NATUR	NEGATIV	POSITIV	PARADE
PAUSE	PERIODE	PLANET	RELATIV
RELIGION	SANDALE	SYMBOL	MOTOR
PERSON	TYP		

Tipp

Insgesamt solltest du 4-mal -e gestrichen und 5-mal -e hinzugefügt haben.

32. **Schreibe zu jedem Wort eines der Betonungsmuster.**

a) Alternativen: oO / Oo.

Von einem der Betonungsmuster gibt es hier nur zwei Beispiele. **Tipp**

action _______	control _______	contact _______
planet _______	guitar _______	legend _______
nature _______	patient _______	sandal _______
perfume _______		

b) Hier ist die Auswahl größer.

Ein Betonungsmuster kommt mit 5-mal am häufigsten vor. **Tipp**

Die Alternativen: oOoo / oOo / Ooo / oO / Oo

vehicle _______	technique _______	passenger _______
miserable _______	gallery _______	direction _______
biology _______	difference _______	period _______

33. **In den Lücken sollst du dir den Laut [k] vorstellen. Füge die richtigen Buchstaben ein. Die Zahl der Buchstaben, die du eingefügt hast, ist durch fünf teilbar. Zwei der Buchstaben kommen nur je einmal vor.**

__ristian	bus__er	__able	__ristmas
__ara__ter	ele__troni__	pani__	te__ni__ue

34. **Wenn du die richtigen Buchstaben für die Lücken aussuchst, kannst du mit den Lösungsbuchstaben herausfinden, wo der größte See der Welt liegt.**

a__ident	cc – C	cs - M	
e__pect	xs – E	x - A	
e__ape	xc – X	sc - N	
e__ecution	x – A	cs - I	
e__pecially	s – D	x - C	
su__essful	cs – O	cc - A	Lösung: ________________

35. In jeder Zeile gibt es zwei Wörter mit dem Laut [z], wie in *zoo* / *music*, und ein Wort ohne diesen Laut. Die Wörter ohne [z] ergeben mit den Lösungsbuchstaben die (englische) Antwort auf die Frage: Welches Landsäugetier hat das beste Gehör?

B	conversation	**D**	example	**A**	opposite
O	choose	**A**	expensive	**P**	organize
E	design	**G**	quiz	**T**	December

36. **Bei diesen Wörtern fehlt der Laut [z] bzw. [gz].**

Wenn du die Buchstaben richtig einsetzt, findest du die Antwort auf diese Scherzfrage: Ein Mann hörte, dass 90 % aller Unfälle in einem Umkreis von 15 km von zu Hause passieren. Was machte er?

bu__iness	s	M	z	S
cra__y	s	L	z	O
e__ample	x	V	xs	E
Mu__lim	s	E	z	P
pri__on	z	T	s	D
la__y	z	H	s	L
ea__ier	z	A	s	O
noi__y	z	T	s	U
suppo__e	s	S	z	E
e__actly	cs	R	x	E

He __ __ __ __ __   __ __ __ __ __ .

37. *Which famous American actor died aged 24 in 1955?* Hier fehlen überall die Buchstaben, die den Laut [ʃ] (wie in *sh*op, wi*sh*) repräsentieren. Als Alternativen stehen dir „ti" und „sh" zur Verfügung. Trifft beides nicht zu, dann schreibst du den Lösungsbuchstaben unter „anderes".

	ti	sh	anderes
B: ▼ugar			*B*
D: pu▼		*D*	
J: ac▼on	*J*		
O: discu▼ion			
E: fla▼			
A: communica▼on			
G: espe▼ially			
M: instruc▼on			
A: Spani▼			
E: men▼on			
A: deli▼ious			
S: pa▼ient			
R: ▼ure			
N: Wel▼			
T: A▼ian			

Tipp

Noch ein anderer bekannter amerikanischer Schauspieler steckt in diesem Rätsel. Er ist durch einen Film bekannt geworden, der in einer großen Stadt in Nordafrika spielte, und danach auch benannt wurde.

38. Unterstreiche den Laut [s] in diesen Wörtern. Nicht jedes Wort hat einen; trotzdem gibt es genauso viele [s] Laute, wie es Wörter gibt.

smell	such	astronaut	success	phrase
replace	Muslim	space	nose	

39. Halte das Gleichgewicht!
Die Lücken enthalten immer den Laut [s], der aber unterschiedlich geschrieben wird. S = 1 kg; C = 2 kg

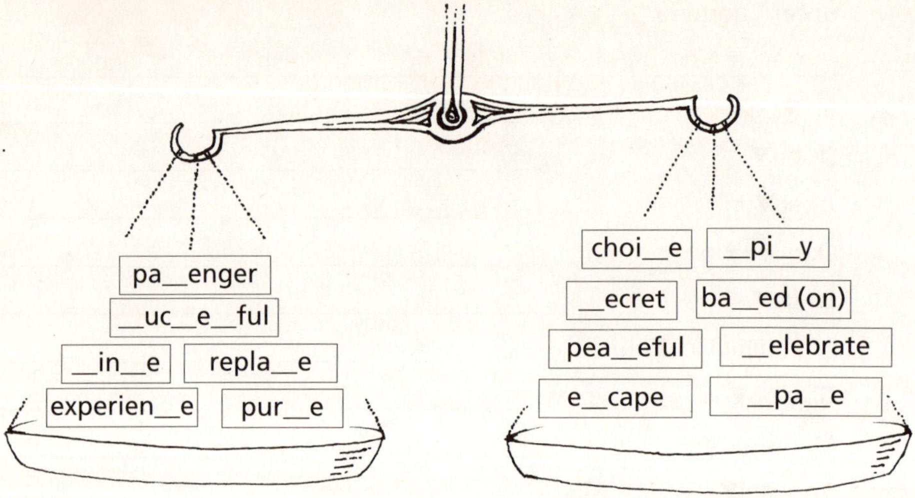

Tipp Am Ende müsste die Waage 15 Kilo auf jeder Seite haben.

40. Diese Wörter enden alle mit der Laut-Kombination [əs]. Welches in jeder Reihe unterscheidet sich in der Schreibweise dieses Lautes von den anderen beiden?

a) homel__ pal__ busin__

b) fam__ delici__ helpl__

c) waitr__ nerv__ danger__

41. Mit der richtigen Endung kannst du einige Rekorde erfahren:

a) Alter des jüngsten Schachmeisters
b) Alter des jüngsten Spielers in einem Endspiel der Fußballweltmeisterschaft
c) Alter des jüngsten Goldmedalliengewinners in der Leichtathletik
d) Alter der jüngsten internationalen Turnerin
e) Alter des / der jüngsten Wimbledon Gewinner(in)
f) Größte Zahl der überlebenden Kinder einer Geburt
g) Alter des ältesten Mannes aller Zeiten
h) Alter der ältesten Menschen aller Zeiten
i) Alter des / der jüngsten Hochschulabsolvent(in)
j) Alter des jüngsten Menschen, der den Mount Everest bestiegen hat
k) Größe der kürzesten Frau aller Zeiten, gemessen mit 9 Jahren (in Zentimetern)
l) Zahl der meisten Kinder von einer Mutter
m) Höhe des größten Schneemannes (in Metern)

		-er	-ar	re	-or	-our
a)	harb-	13	17	15	16	14
b)	ent-	17	14	18	20	15
c)	doct-	12	14	16	15	13
d)	gramm-	10	9	12	11	14
e)	sug-	17	15	14	16	19
f)	centimet-	6	8	7	5	9
g)	off-	120	119	121	122	118
h)	busk-	122	123	125	127	130
i)	operat-	12	17	16	10	15
j)	doll-	16	17	18	13	20
k)	mirr-	54	60	56	55	59
l)	neighb-	39	27	36	67	69
m)	simil-	11	34	25	14	36

G Übungsdiktate 2

1. Plural-s; 3. Person Singular-s

Toby belongs to a sports club ˈ and he goes to taekwondo* training ˈ oOo
twice a week. He enjoys it, and he knows ˈ that he can easily beat
anybody ˈ who attacks him. The trainer teaches the group ˈ new
techniques* ˈ and they practise on each other. They have to know oO
the names ˈ of different sorts of kicks ˈ and ways of using ˈ their hands
and arms. Every six months there's a test. At the moment, Toby has
a yellow belt, and if he passes the next test ˈ he'll be allowed to wear
a green one. There are usually lots of parents ˈ and other relatives* ˈ Ooo
at the test. Toby's dad cheers and claps with the others ˈ when the
belts are given out.

(117 words)

2. Plural-s; 3. Person Singular-s (Fortsetzung)

On Monday evenings ˈ Toby catches* the bus to the sports hall, but Oo
on Thursdays ˈ his dad drives him there, and stays and watches* ˈ Oo
for a few minutes, unless he's in a hurry. He takes a real interest* ˈ Oo
in the ideas behind taekwondo*, and supports Toby in every way. oOo
He sees it as part of his son's education*. Toby's mum doesn't want ooOo
to learn the mysteries* ˈ of the sport. She's glad that Toby is learning Ooo
it, though she doesn't understand ˈ why he has to learn foreign* ['fɒrən]
phrases ˈ and count up to ten in a different language. Toby has
explained that it's useful ˈ in international* competitions*, ooOo – ooOo
but his mum secretly hopes ˈ that he won't get that far.

(115 words)

3. Plural-s; 3. Person Singular-s

In English lessons, Mr Norton sometimes discusses* ˈ different oOo
sorts of books ˈ with the pupils. He agrees with them ˈ that films
are important, but he believes ˈ that books are better. The boys
seem to like horror stories ˈ about monsters, robbers and thieves*. O
They're happiest ˈ when the heroes* beat their enemies*, and if ['hi:rəʊz] Ooo
an enemy dies ˈ that just adds to the fun. The girls enjoy mysteries ˈ
and love stories, or books about horses. The best ones are a
combination* ˈ of all three. Almost all the children in Form 9a ˈ also ooOo
like books of facts, records and the results of interesting surveys*. ['sɜ:veɪz]

(98 words)

4. Genitiv-s

Jane has got quite a few books about cooking. She likes
making meals, especially* curries, and she enjoys finding oOo
out the differences* ˈ between spices. Her family's favourite Ooo
meal ˈ is chicken curry, and when Jane's mum is at the ladies'
fitness class ˈ on Tuesday evenings, Jane cooks for the others.
Alfie's job is to set the table. He usually watches a children's
TV programme* ˈ called 'Kids' Hour' ˈ at this time, and it's Oo
usually about people's work or hobbies. For example, today
they are at a vet's surgery, and next week's programme ˈ will
be about police* dogs and police horses, one of Jane's
favourite topics. She'll be cooking something quick and easy
that day: eggs on toast.

(115 words)

5. Plural-s und Genitiv-s

This term, one of Form 9a's teachers has planned a project ˈ
which compares* towns and cities. Five groups will find out ˈ oO
about different areas of interest. Daniel and four of his
classmates ˈ have to report* on ethnic* groups in the city. They oO – ['eθnɪk]
have found a magazine article ˈ about the problems foreigners* ['fɒrənəz]
may have in Britain, and about British people's attitudes* ˈ to Ooo
different religions* and languages. Two surveys were carried oOo
out, and the results were not very surprising. Almost everybody
enjoys Indian curries ˈ and other foreign dishes, but Hindus,
for example, have problems with their neighbours' attitudes*. ['ætɪtju:dz]

(94 words)

6. Plural-s, 3. Person Singular-s und Genitiv-s

There are Indians working in most British industries* ˈ and Ooo
businesses*. Take the railways, for example. Most of the ['bɪznəsɪz]
managers and engineers* are white men, while many of the ooO
lower paid jobs ˈ are taken by Pakistanis*. They check passengers' ooOo
tickets, make sandwiches* in snack bars ˈ and clean the stations. ['sænwɪdʒɪz]
Balia is in her thirties, and she looks after the ladies' toilets ˈ
at a station in a big city. If there is a problem*, she fixes it, but Oo
she often gets bored. Her children cook for themselves ˈ when
she is at work. She wishes she could have her cousin's* job. ['kʌznz]
This cousin works at a doctor's surgery*. Many Indian nurses ['sɜ:dʒərɪ]
and doctors ˈ work in British surgeries and hospitals*. Ooo

(116 words)

7. *-ing*-Form und *simple past / past participle*

Kennst du den „Fantastic Mr Fox", von Roald Dahl? Die nächsten fünf Diktate sind eine verkürzte Version dieser Geschichte.

There was once a very clever fox ˈ who lived in a hole ˈ with his
wife and his four little foxes. The three farmers in the area hated
him, and chasing him ˈ was one of their favourite activities*. They oOoo
often argued* ˈ about the best way to catch him, and in the end ˈ ['ɑ:gju:d]
they arranged to wait with their guns ˈ outside his hole one evening.
'He has robbed our farms for long enough,' they agreed. 'Our
chickens are being caught, killed and eaten, and that fox has
always managed to escape. Our lives are being controlled by
him and his family. This must not be allowed to continue!'

(104 words)

8. *-ing*-Form und *simple past / past participle*

That night, Mr Fox decided to leave the hole ˈ and find some
food ˈ at one of the farms. As soon as the air touched* his nose, [tʌtʃt]
he smelled the three farmers ˈ who were lying on the ground.
He turned round quickly ˈ and escaped back down the hole, but
one of the farmers managed to shoot. When Mr Fox entered
the hole again, his tail was missing. His children cried, and
his wife thought he was dying. At first she panicked. Then
she cleaned him up ˈ and covered the place which hurt ˈ with a cloth.
While she was tying it up, her husband wondered ˈ what to do next.

(108 words)

9. *-ing*-Form und *simple past / past participle*

The whole family was getting hungrier every hour. Mr Fox offered to leave the hole again, but the whole family voted against ˈ such a dangerous plan.

'You almost died last time,' said Mrs Fox. 'We may be hungry, but at least we're safe here. Please don't go.'

The farmers were also wondering ˈ what to do. One of them ˈ mentioned the idea of plugging the hole ˈ with earth, filling it in ˈ so that the foxes had no way of escaping. But the others disagreed*. 'He'll just come out somewhere else,' they pointed out. 'Digging him out will be better.'

(96 words)

10. *-ing*-Form und *simple past / past participle*

Soon the foxes heard machines* ˈ above their heads. The foxes oO
started to dig into the hill, and managed to keep away ˈ from the
men. It got dark outside, and the farmers stopped digging ˈ for that
day. One of them stayed and watched the hole.
All night, while his children slept, Mr Fox concentrated* on ways Oooo
of finding food. Slowly, an idea began to form in his mind.
'Hiding here won't help,' he said to his wife. 'We must dig again.
Don't worry, my darling. I have a wonderful plan.'
On the next day, he and the children started digging again.
Mrs Fox stayed behind. She was much too tired and hungry to help.
(113 words)

11. *-ing*-Form und *simple past / past participle*

Mr Fox didn't tell the children ˈ what he was planning, but at last
they reached the place ˈ he hoped to find.
'We are going to climb* up here ˈ into the chicken house ˈ of one [klaɪm]
of the farms,' he explained, 'and take as many chickens ˈ as we
can carry. They will be cooked, and a party will be held ˈ for
all the animals.'
You can imagine* ˈ how excited* the children were. They oOo – oOo
killed a lot of chickens ˈ and took vegetables* for the rabbits, [ˈvedʒtəblz]
and carried everything back ˈ to their mother. Soon all the
animals were celebrating* their success*. Mr Fox was a Oooo – oO
hero, ˈ and everybody cheered and clapped ˈ when they
heard the story ˈ of his exciting adventures*. oOo
(120 words)

12. *Gerunds*

Jane would like to write to somebody ˈ of her own age ˈ in a
different part of the country*. A few weeks ago ˈ she wrote to [ˈkʌntri]
a girls' magazine* ˈ with a list of her hobbies: cooking, reading, ooO
cycling, playing the piano and, of course, writing letters. Her
letter was printed, and a few girls and boys have written to her.
One girl says ˈ that although* she is frightened of flying, she flies oO
to Germany every winter ˈ with her family and goes skiing* ˈ in the [ˈskiːɪŋ]
mountains. She enjoys skating, dancing and windsurfing. In her
spare time ˈ she enjoys listening to classical music ˈ and playing chess.
(103 words)

13. *Gerunds* und andere *-ing*-Formen

One of Jane's letters ˈ is from a boy called Andrew. He plays the piano, too, but he doesn't like practising, and he's thinking of giving it up. He likes going swimming ˈ and taking the family's dog for walks. He's very interested in writing to a girl, because he's got three brothers ˈ and no sisters. Jane was hoping ˈ to find somebody ˈ with exactly the same hobbies as herself, but although* Andrew has completely different hobbies, oO
he sounds like a nice boy, so she is definitely going to write to him.
(89 words)

14. Steigerung auf -er / -est

Janes erster Brief an Andrew:

Dear Andrew,
Thanks for your letter. Are you the youngest in your family? I've got one younger brother. He's tall for his age, but I'm still bigger and stronger than him. With visitors he's the nicest, politest* child you could wish for, but really he's the craziest oOo
person ˈ in the family. He says that I'm lazier than he is, because I get up later than him at weekends. That's true, but I'm also much busier than he is. I like cooking hot, spicy curries – the hotter and spicier, the better. My mother says ˈ she has become lazier but healthier* ˈ since I started ['helθɪə]
cooking. My dad is getting fatter. Well, it's certainly cheaper ˈ than eating in a restaurant*,and it's more fun, too. Write Oo
soon, and tell me more about yourself.
Yours, Jane.
(132 words)

15. Steigerung auf -er / -est; Adverbien auf -ly

Dear Jane,
I was really pleased to get your letter yesterday. In answer to
your question, I've got one older brother ˈ and two younger ones.
None of us is very quiet, but those two are the noisiest of all.
Fortunately*, they are still sleeping peacefully. I usually get up — Ooo [ˈfɔːtʃnətli]
earlier ˈ than they do, because it's much easier to concentrate* — Ooo
properly* ˈ when they are not around. — Ooo
I have seen on the map exactly ˈ where you live. It's nearly a
hundred miles away, but it's a relatively easy journey by train.
I love all sorts of curries, especially hot ones, but our meals
are mostly boring. My dad has to keep strictly to low-fat food ˈ
without any salt, because he has problems with his heart*. — [hɑːt]
May I visit you next week?
Love, Andrew.
(131 words)

16. Adverbien auf -ly

Jane showed Andrew's letter to her parents. Her mum smiled.
'I can just imagine him sitting miserably at the table ˈ in
front of his boring meal,' she said, 'and patiently waiting
for an invitation from you.'
Jane decided to tell him politely* but clearly ˈ that his idea — oOo
was a bit crazy.
'I would gladly cook a curry for you,' she wrote, 'but it
must be one of the longest journeys ˈ anybody has ever made,
just for a meal. Why don't you just buy a book about cooking?
Your father can still eat healthily. Most curries are low in salt
and fat, and they taste much more interesting ˈ than traditional* — oOo
British food*. Try it, and let me know ˈ if it turns out successfully*.' — [fuːd] – oOoo
(120 words)

17. Apostrophe

Three of Toby's grandparents* are still alive. One grandfather ['grænpeərənts]
lives in the same town ˈ as Toby and his parents. He's Toby's
dad's father. Since his wife's death* ˈ some years ago, he has [deθ]
lived alone. In his house ˈ there's a clock as tall as a man. Its
tick is terribly loud, but luckily, Toby's grandfather can't hear it.
He can't hear the doorbell, either, but Toby has got a key*. [ki:]
'Has today's newspaper come?' he asks, when Toby comes to
visit him ˈ at ten o'clock ˈ one Saturday morning. The neighbours* ['neɪbəz]
also have a newspaper, and Toby has just seen the newspaper
boy's bike ˈ outside their house.
'It'll be here any minute,' he shouts in his grandfather's
ear. 'I'll go and get it.'

(121 words)

18. Apostrophe

Toby's mother's parents live with their son and his wife,
Toby's uncle and aunt, on their farm. Until a few years ago ˈ
it was Toby's grandparents' farm, but his uncle and aunt
have been running it ˈ since their marriage*. Toby usually ['mærɪdʒ]
has a week's holiday there ˈ in the summer. He likes to listen
to his grandmother's stories.
'Children these days are lucky, aren't they?' she says.
'We had to get up at five o'clock ˈ and help in the fields ˈ
or feed the cows ˈ before school. And then we had half* an [hɑ:f]
hour's walk ˈ to the village. When the road was blocked by
snow ˈ we had to stay at home.'
'You're right, of course,' answers her husband, 'but I'm sure
Toby won't want to hear ˈ our old stories of past times.'

(130 words)

19. Groß- und Kleinschreibung

Fabian's Aunt Paula and Uncle Fred ˈ are doing some
sightseeing in London, the capital* city of the UK. They've Ooo
decided not to take ˈ an organized tour, because this way they
will be free ˈ to choose their own route*. They definitely want [ru:t]
to see Buckingham Palace*. They think it looks quite similar* to Oo – ['sɪmɪlə]
Ludwig's palaces* in Bavaria. Then there's the Tower of Ooo
London, of course, and Trafalgar Square with its statues of
lions ˈ around a central monument*. The British Museum* and Ooo – oOo
the National* Gallery* ˈ are also on their list, because Fred loves Oo – Ooo
museums ˈ and Paula is interested in modern* art. Oo

(98 words)

20. Groß- und Kleinschreibung

Later, Fred and Paula are sitting in a pub ˈ called the *Dish*
and Spoon. They're German, so they don't understand* ˈ the ooO
reason for the name ˈ until the owner explains it to them. He
says there's an English children's song ˈ which ends like this:
'The dish ran away with the spoon.' Although* English food* oO – [fu:d]
is supposed* to be boring, there are some delicious* smells ˈ in oO – oOo
this pub. Paula is looking at the choice of salads* ˈ on the menu*. Oo – Oo
Fred is reading a newspaper ˈ called the *Evening News*.
'Order some Spanish white wine,' he says to his wife, 'and
fish and chips for me.'
Paula has a special* request*. She wants a green salad, Oo – oO
but without the French dressing.
(117 words)

21. Groß- und Kleinschreibung; Getrennt- und Zusammenschreibung

There's some very interesting news in the newspaper. Some
astronauts* are on their way to Mars. It's the most exciting Ooo
event ˈ in space travel ˈ since the moon landing in 1969. That's
Fred's opinion*, anyway. He would love to go into space oOo
himself, but the tourist industry* ˈ doesn't offer space travel yet. Ooo
'I expect that booking a trip to another planet* ˈ will soon be Oo
just like buying ˈ a plane ticket to New York,' he says. 'Look
at this newspaper article*. It says that there are canyons on Mars, Ooo
much bigger than the Grand Canyon in America. Some of them
are so straight ˈ that they could be canals*. These astronauts oO
are going to look for signs of life there.'
(117 words)

22. Groß- und Kleinschreibung; Getrennt- und Zusammenschreibung

Fred is combining his holiday in Britain ˈ with a business* trip, so Oo
he has to spend Monday morning ˈ at some offices* in the city centre. Ooo
Paula is pushing her way through the crowds ˈ in a department* oOo
store ˈ which sells everything ˈ from egg sandwiches to exercise
cycles. She's looking for Christmas presents* ˈ for her relatives. Oo
She chooses toy cars for Paul, a Russian doll for Jasmin ˈ and a
microphone* for Fabian. She also buys some gold coins ˈ made Ooo
out of milk chocolate*. Choosing suitable* gifts for adults ˈ is Oo – ['su:təbl]
more difficult. In the end ˈ she buys some Indian tea, some
perfume*and a film ˈ called Pearl Harbor*. It is a special offer, Oo – ['hɑ:bə]
so she is very careful ˈ to take the price label off!
(121 words)

23. Ähnliche Wörter im Deutschen und Englischen

Robert and his mum ˈ are at a large railway station. Passengers
are walking and running ˈ in all directions* ˈ to buy tickets or — oOo
catch trains. Robert notices differences ˈ in skin colour and
clothes*. Some clearly belong to unusual* religions*. He can — O – oOo – oOo
see two men ˈ with very short hair, strange yellow clothes and
sandals*. They are speaking a foreign* language ˈ and they — Oo – ['fɒrən]
look Chinese*. Here is a disabled* woman ˈ in an electric — oO – oOo
wheelchair, a very useful little vehicle* ˈ with a motor ˈ which — Ooo ['vi:əkl]
can be controlled with two fingers. She is following arrows ˈ
with the wheelchair symbol*, because she knows ˈ there will — Oo
be lifts and ramps ˈ on this route.

(106 words)

24. Ähnliche Wörter im Deutschen und Englischen

Robert and his mum were going to London ˈ to watch a parade*. — oO
They arrived at the central station early, so they watched a
busker ˈ near the main entrance. Robert plays the guitar* — oO
himself, but this young man's technique* was brilliant. He had — oO
an electric guitar, with a cable ˈ which led to a black box. Robert
could have stayed there for hours, but his mum wanted to buy a
newspaper ˈ with an article* about last night's bomb* attack ˈ in — Ooo – [bɒm]
Ireland. Some of the books at the newsagent's ˈ had interesting
titles. Robert wanted to buy one ˈ about Viking* legends*, but — ['vaɪkɪŋ] – Oo
his mum pointed out ˈ that it was really too big to carry ˈ
around London all day.

(114 words)

25. Ähnliche Wörter im Deutschen und Englischen

Do you ever pause*, and wonder ˈ what type of person* you are? — [pɔ:z] – Oo
Do you like lots of action, or do you have a quiet, peaceful
nature? Are you good in an emergency*, or do you — oOoo
panic? Are you patient*? Are you good at making — ['peɪʃnt]
contact* ˈ with others? Can you control your feelings? Are you — Oo
miserable ˈ when something goes wrong, or do you
just think ˈ it's all good experience? There are positive and
negative things ˈ about everybody's character*, and people — Ooo
can change ˈ from one period* of their lives to another. — Ooo

(89 words)

26. Ähnlich klingende Wörter: *spend – spent; piece – peace; although – also; bored – board*

When Iris is bored, she practises the keyboard. Although* oO
she has only just started having lessons, the time she has
spent practising ˈ is already showing results. She would like
to spend more time on it, but sometimes her mother wants ˈ
some peace and quiet, so she leaves it for another day. Her
favourite piece is one called 'Yellow River'.
She can make the sounds of different instruments*, such Ooo
as the harp, the guitar* or the piano, just by pressing the oO
right button. There is also a button marked 'French horn',
but it sounds more like a cow in pain.
(99 words)

27. Ähnlich klingende Wörter: *rich – reach; fax – facts;* verschiedene Vokabeln

Toby's parents are not rich, but they have enough money,
so his mum doesn't go to work. She is a good Christian,
and when she read an advert* ˈ asking for volunteers* at a Oo – ooO
day centre ˈ for homeless men and women* in the city, she ['wɪmɪn]
sent a fax ˈ requesting more information*. Soon after that, ooOo
a letter arrived with facts, figures and a small map with
instructions ˈ about how to reach the centre.
'It's a good cause,' she explained to her husband and son, 'and
I feel useless here at home ˈ all day. I spend my time between
the fridge, the oven* and the kitchen sink, or I pick up a [ʌvn]
catalogue* ˈ and choose clothes* ˈ which I don't need. I feel Ooo – O
that God has called me to do this work.'
(128 words)

28. Vokabeln

At the centre, two ladies made Toby's mum welcome ˈ and
offered her a cup of tea. Suddenly, she wasn't hungry or
thirsty. There was a funny smell in the building, and it
seemed to be overheated. The homeless men looked at her ˈ
without saying anything. They looked as if they had just
come out of prison, and she quietly put a hand on the
pocket ˈ where her purse* was. She didn't feel ˈ that she could [pɜ:s]
care for these people at all, and wished that she was back at
home. The ladies explained ˈ how to operate the microwave ˈ
and the dishwasher*, and asked if she would like ˈ to Ooo
take tea to the men ˈ and get to know them.
(117 words)

29. Vokabeln

'Hello, I'm Mrs Brown,' she said to a man ˈ who looked less
dirty than the others. 'Do you take sugar* in your tea?' ['ʃʊgə]
'Are you the new volunteer*?' he asked, without looking at ooO
her. 'You won't stay long. They never do. It's a dump, that's what it is.'
In her heart*, she agreed with him. Somebody was playing a [hɑ:t]
sad tune ˈ on a cassette* player. Through the window ˈ the view oO
included a grey wall ˈ which was covered in graffiti*. There oOo
was no way of escaping the smell. She thought ˈ it must be
the saddest place ˈ in the whole of the British Isles*. She [aɪlz]
could feel tears* in her eyes, and hurried back to the [tɪəs]
kitchen ˈ before anybody noticed ˈ that she was crying.

(122 words)

30. Vokabeln

A lot of foreigners live and work in Britain, but they
have kept their own religions*, languages and festivals*. oOo – Ooo
Muslims, Hindus and Christians live side by side ˈ in the
big cities. The Hindu people have a festival ˈ when they
light lamps in their homes ˈ and eat special* food. You ['speʃl]
can often hear people speaking Urdu*, an Indian language, ['ʊədu:]
in the street, and some of the older women ˈ never really
learn English properly, so communication* with their English oooOo
neighbours ˈ can be a problem*. Oo

(82 words)

31. Vokabeln

One of the oldest languages in the British Isles* ˈ is Welsh. For [aɪlz]
a time, it seemed to be dying out, but the people of Wales ˈ
didn't want it to be completely replaced* ˈ by English. Now oO
the road signs in Wales ˈ are written in both languages, and
Welsh is also taught in schools. This means ˈ that old poems
and songs ˈ will still be read and understood. If you watch the
news on TV in Wales, you may see what is happening ˈ from
the pictures on the screen, but you won't understand the
presenter. The grammar of Welsh ˈ is not at all like English
grammar, and very few English people can speak the language.
They don't need to; after all, English is spoken everywhere.

(122 words)

32. Vokabeln

Toby's grandfather is an artist*, but he doesn't paint. He — Oo
makes collages* | with pieces of old magazines*. He and — ['kɒlɑːʒɪz] – ooO
some other artists | have organized a show | which is open
to the public*. When Toby went to see it, he went straight — Oo
to the section | with the collages. One of them had a red
spot below it. That was a code | which meant that it was sold.
He looked at the name | at the bottom of the picture | and
saw that it was his grandfather's.
'It was bought by a rich American* tourist* | for one — oOoo – Oo
hundred dollars,' said his grandfather later.
He pulled the money out of his pocket | and counted
it again. He couldn't believe his luck.
(126 words)

33. Vokabeln

This story is based on a fairy story | about a princess
and a frog. There was once a beautiful princess | who
often played with a golden ball | at the edge of a pool |
in the palace gardens. The pool was so still | that she
could see her face in it, just like a mirror. One day,
her ball fell into the pool | and sank out of sight. She
was in a very unhappy mood, because it was her favourite
toy, and she guessed* | that her father would not drain the — [gest]
pool for her. But a frog spoke to her.
'Don't worry, princess! I will find your ball for you. But
first you must promise | to let me eat from your plate |
and sleep in your bed.'
(126 words)

34. Vokabeln

The girl was sure | that the frog could not follow her |
into the palace*, so she promised him what he requested. — ['pæləs]
A few moments* later, he appeared with the ball. She took — Oo
it from him | and without even thanking him, ran off down
the path. While she and her father and sisters | were having
dinner, there was a knock* at the door. It was the frog, of — [nɒk]
course, and he explained why he was there. The king told
his daughter to do what the frog asked, because a promise
has to be kept. She shook her head miserably. She could not
be a slave or a friend | to this cold, wet animal.
(112 words)

35. Vokabeln

The frog ate from her plate, but she could not eat anything. Then she had to carry him up to her bedroom. She could feel his bones through the skin – horrible! Once the door was closed, she threw the frog into a corner, with tears in her eyes. After a few minutes, the frog climbed* into her bed with her. ['klaɪmd] She decided to leave him there, because she didn't want to touch him again. Suddenly there was a brilliant flash of light, and the frog disappeared. A kind, smiling prince with beautiful clothes | appeared in his place.

(97 words)

36. Vokabeln

'Sorry about that,' said the prince. 'I was turned into a frog | by a terrible old woman. I could only become a man again | if a beautiful young princess | let me share her life with her. Thank you for saving me. I hope you're not going | to ask your father to execute* me now,' he added Ooo with a smile.

The princess was very surprised, but she kept a cool head | and invited him to the palace barbecue | on the next day. There, he asked her to marry him, and they lived happily ever after.

(94 words)

Lösungen

A Die Lautschrift

1. **a)** tree – **b)** job – **c)** shelf – **d)** shook – **e)** zoo – **f)** through › *Seite 8*
Joke: eat – drink – laziest – translate – week – work

2. **a)** then – **b)** check – **c)** choose – **d)** five – **e)** wine – **f)** eleven › *Seite 9*
Joke: slow – front – faster – allowed – leave

3. **a)** fat – **b)** what – **c)** Andy – **d)** sung – **e)** easy – **f)** party
Joke: farm – showed – means – running – socks

4. **a)** good – **b)** you – **c)** drove – **d)** found – **e)** begun – **f)** light › *Seite 10*
Joke: kitchen – quickly – empty plate – brother – angrily – why – hurried

B Words in context 1

1. **Gregory:** false – opinions – even – programmes – important – else › *Seite 11*
Tom: ever – skate – Christmas – helmet – nervous – jewellery – youth – grow
Rebecca: enough – etc. – completely – short – dialogue – able

2. Die Antwort bezieht sich auf Rebeccas Brief. › *Seite 12*

3. **a)** etc. **b)** usw.

4. [f]: false – enough; [v]: even – ever – nervous

5. [s]: false – else – skate – Christmas – nervous – etc.

6. **a)** ● false □ falls **b)** falls … false › *Seite 13*

7. **a)** ▽ board ▼ bought **b)** bought … board

8. OPINION**CHILDREN**ELSE**SHOULD**NERVOUS**BE**ENOUGH
SEENEVEN**AND**CHRISTMAS**NOT**YOUTH**HEARD**!
Kinder soll man sehen und nicht hören!

9. drama – autumn – copied – actor – Christmas – other – actress – dad – cameras – following – happened – organize – character – article – photo – heroes – stop – combination – improve – factory – studied – plans – interview › *Seite 14*

10. **a)** article – photo **b)** characters **c)** drama **d)** interview **e)** plan **f)** stop **g)** copy › *Seite 15*

11. autumn (stummes n); Christmas (stummes t) › *Seite 16*

12. actor – autumn – factory – organize

13. heroes; photo

14. **a)** ⌘ side ❁ sight **b)** side – side – sight

15. **a)** ◆ your ◇ you're **b)** you're – your – you're – your › *Seite 17*

16. *autumn* ist korrekt geschrieben. Das kürzeste Theaterstück dauert 30 Sekunden. Die anderen Wörter korrigiert: *actress*, *Christmas*, *character*.

17. Europeans – pavement – reach – grew up – sold – rescued – activities – scary – empty – smuggling – washes – factory – hours – sell – study – design – Europe – receive – heads › *Seite 18*

18. Europe – European – rescued › *Seite 19*

19. design (stummes g); hours (stummes h)

20. reach – believe – leave – receive – activities; Anders ist *receive* mit *-ei-* nach c.
Der Regel heißt: *i before e, except after c.*

21. **a)** sell **b)** smuggle **c)** activity **d)** wash **e)** rescue **f)** grow up

Seite 20 ‹

22. a) ◆ made ◇ mate b) mate – mate – made

23. It is the most CROWDED city in the world.

24. suitcase – dictionary – map – journeys – travel – toilets – boat – above – conversation – slow – bacon – exchange – choir – combined – souvenirs – concert – religious – popular – cassette – whistling

Seite 22 ‹

25. a) Ooo b) oOo c) ooO d) ooOo

26. cassette – bacon – combined – concert – popular – souvenirs

27. whistle (stummes h, stummes t)

28. [ʃ]: dictionary; conversation; [dʒ]: journeys; religious; exchange

29. suitcase – religious – dictionary – popular – choir – journey

Seite 23 ‹

30. a) ✻ mouse ∗ mouth b) mouse – mouth

31. a) ▶ here ◁ hear b) hear – here

32. Holly and her friends are in the SOUTH of France. (choir: group of people who sing…; dictionary: a book …; slow: opp. of quick; conversation: exchange of ideas…; above: opp. of below

Seite 24 ‹

33. received – healthy – suitable – jacket – horse – straight – cricket – slow – grown – calendar – hockey – sailing – motor – cycling – engine – life – skiing – queue – flight – tall – reach – metre – proof – special – unit – national – opinion – noisy – exercise

Seite 26 ‹

34. a) metre – reach – received – skiing
b) You need a key to open a door. Have a piece of cake.

35. a) calendar – metre – motor b) summer / winter; idea

36. a) grown b) flight c) horse d) straight e) slow

37. proof – queue – suitable

38. a) national – special b) shout

Seite 27 ‹

39. a) ◆ two ▲ too b) two – too – too

40. Jamie also plays GOLF. Die Wörter sind: proof; engine; opinion; healthy.

41. thought – divorced – quite – articles – situation; disco – kisses; imagine; king – free – Queen – even – suitable; Detectives – activities – silly; bathroom – knock; people – special – famous – born; example; type – popular – including

Seite 29 ‹

42. imagine oOo; activities oOoo; popular Ooo; famous Oo; including oOo; detectives oOo; divorced oO; situation ooOo; special Oo; suitable Ooo; articles Ooo

43. knock

44. article – kiss – put – detective – activity – repair – include

45. a) ◆ hole ✻ whole b) hole – whole

46. a) △ son ▽ sun b) son – sun – sun

Seite 30 ‹

47. Prince William … was rugby and hockey TEAM CAPTAIN.

48. candle – packet – festival – weather – trousers – frightened – telephone – ambulance – disabled – authentic – special – head – pilot – entrance – slogan – sign – office – corridor – labels – technology – statue – ridden

Seite 32 ‹

49. technology oOoo; packet Oo; pilot Oo; frightened Oo; special Oo

50. pilot – frightened – sign

51. sign; design

Seite 33 ‹

52. festival – label – candle; [l]; 3

53. a) left – passed – stopped – passed – drove – passed – was – have passed – know.
Das Wort *passed* ist ein Verb, während *past* kein Verb ist.
b) ✻ past ▼ passed c) past – past – passed – past – past – passed – past.

54. a) ◆ road ◇ rode b) rode – rode – road – road › Seite 34

55. a) △ allowed ▶ a loud b) allowed – a loud – a loud – allowed

56. a) [laɪf]: for life / there's life; [lɪv]: to live;
b) *live* ist ein Verb und *life* ist ein Nomen.
c) ■ live □ life
d) life – live – life – live – live – live – life

57. CANDLE**AN**ENTRANCE**ANGRY**PILOT**HORSE**
AMBULANCE**PUTS**TELEPHONE**ITS**HEAD**EARS**STATUE**BACK** › Seite 35

C Word workshop 1

1. a) 2; b) 2; c) 2; d) 2; e) 3; f) 1; g) 2; h) 1; i) 3; j) 4; k) 3; l) 1 › Seite 36

2. a) waitresses b) accidents c) prizes d) garages e) ghosts f) dishes
g) keys h) sizes i) concerts j) entrances k) forests l) matches
m) wishes n) buses o) churches

3. a) emergency b) body c) diary

4. a) factories b) assemblies c) ferries d) dictionaries e) activities f) hobbies › Seite 37

5. a) boy b) holiday c) ways d) journeys e) toys

6. a) kindergartens
b) rucksacks
c) hobbies

7. b) detective c) concerts d) programme e) situations f) cassette g) characters
h) article i) tourists j) statue k) farmers l) dialogue m) taxi

8. a) Der Buchstabe **o** fehlt. › Seite 38
b) potatoes; tomatoes; heroes

9. a) families – radios b) factories – cities c) postmen – uniforms – hobbies – budgies
d) journeys – countries e) photos – statues – churches
f) dictionaries – rucksacks – addresses g) potatoes – tomatoes
h) heroes – concerts – matches

10. half – halves; shelf – shelves; wife – wives; life – lives › Seite 39

11. Toby's mother **works** very hard in an office every day. Toby's father usually **washes** the clothes. He **goes** to work, too, but he **does** a lot of his work at home. He always **tries** to be there when Toby **comes** home from school. He **worries** if Toby is late. He **goes** shopping and **buys** most of the food for the family.

12. **linke Spalte:** a) wash b) worry c) do d) try e) copy f) improve g) receive h) grow › Seite 40
rechte Spalte: a) works b) goes c) comes d) rescues e) finishes f) buys g) kisses
h) studies

13. comes – kisses – says – goes – studies – finishes – copies – washes – tries

14. **Unterstrichen:** coming – getting – changing – stopping – driving – overtaking – forgetting – dancing – putting › Seite 41

15. a) make b) drop c) cycle d) write e) pull

16. a) are having b) 's just driving c) was just eating d) is speaking
e) was trying f) were carrying g) is stopping h) I'm writing

17. a) copying b) organize c) agreeing d) travel e) smuggling f) ski › Seite 42
g) cutting h) clap i) sailing j) kiss k) knocking l) sell
m) rescuing n) whistle o) including p) prepare q) repeating r) combine
Die Botschaft: Have a break!

18. a) drop b) carry c) watch d) decide › Seite 43

19. a) 3; b) 2; c) 1; d) 3; e) 2; f) 1; g) 1; h) 2; i) 1; j) 2; k) 1; l) 2

Seite 43 ‹

20. a) exchanged b) included c) kicked d) studied e) travelled f) visited g) clapped h) copied i) designed j) finished k) followed l) owned

21. a) married – husband – called
b) thought – heard – outside
c) friend – found – bird – held
d) said – World – pleased – told – stayed – wanted – spend – allowed
e) cold – ride – decided
f) watched – hundred – stopped
g) disabled – played – frightened – clapped – finished

Seite 44 ‹

22. smallest – empty – bigger – nearly – full;
Adjektive in der Grundform: empty; full. Endungen: -est; -er; -ly

Seite 45 ‹

23. angry; careful; correct; big; funny; noisy; nice

24. a) nervously b) healthily c) kindly d) usually – quietly – noisily e) religiously f) beautifully – slowly g) busily – carefully h) Suddenly – angrily – stupidly i) cheaply

Seite 46 ‹

25. a) hotter b) hottest c) kindest d) funniest e) sunnier f) wetter – wetter g) drier

26. a) noisiest b) cloudier c) nicer d) fitter – fittest – fitter e) latest f) tallest – taller g) earlier h) thinner – thinnest

Seite 47 ‹

27. a) Sg. b) Pl. c) Sg. d) Sg. e) Pl. f) Pl.

28. a) Jane's – Men's Choir's – London's
b) didn't – interviewer's
c) Women's – husband's friends'
d) bird's – Browns'
e) Toby's - week's
f) I'll – hour's – Anne's
g) Stephen's – we've

Seite 48 ‹

29. a) There's b) We're c) They've d) she'll e) I'm – can't f) Don't – it'll g) hasn't h) won't – we've

30. **Today's** the first day back at school after the holidays. **Daniel's** teacher is giving some information to her pupils.
"**There'll** be a **week's** holiday at the beginning of November. On 26th November **it's** the head **teacher's** birthday, and **it's** the **choir's** job to sing a few songs for him. Next week **there's** a table tennis tournament, teachers against pupils. **I'm** playing in that, but I **don't** think **I'll** win. **You're** all too good for me! Oh yes, and the **Parents'** Association wants to hold a jumble sale, so if **you've** got any old toys, **children's** clothes etc., **don't** forget to bring them in two **weeks'** time. **We've** got two football matches against Biddulph High School at the end of October. The **girls'** match is on 29th and the **boys'** match is on 31st, just before the holidays begin. Both matches start at 3 **o'clock**. I'd also like to say that some **pupils'** idea of "on time" **isn't** the same as mine. **I'd** like you to be here at quarter to nine in the morning. If **you're** late, we **can't** get on with the lessons. You really **mustn't** forget that. Now, **I'm** organizing the school play this year, and rehearsals begin next month. **I've** decided **who's** playing the **detective's** part and **who's** playing the **hero's** part, but there are lots of other characters, so I hope **you'll** come to the casting in a **week's** time. Any questions? Well, I think **that's** all for now. **It's** nearly ten **o'clock**. **Let's** get on with the English lesson."

Seite 49 ‹

31. a) **Namens**; Wolstanton High School – North of England; b) **Ländernamen;** British – English; c) **Nomen**; house – apple – tree – garden; d) **kleingeschrieben;** rucksack – kindergarten; e) **großgeschrieben;** Music – History; f) **Feiertagen;** Christmas Day – Boxing Day

Seite 50 ‹

32. a) job – hotel – French – Spanish – European b) tourists – summer – taxi – bus – hotel – rucksack – plan – hand c) American – Asian – European – North of England – Scottish d) South-West – England – sea – west e) doctor – Dr Young – Turkish – rucksack – Europe f) Black Forest – Germany – forest – black g) Germany – Christmas presents – Christmas Eve – Britain – evening – Christmas Day – chocolate – Christmas tree – December – day

33. a) school – (Wolstanton) High School – old street – Old Street **b)** Maths – Geography – hockey – winter – tennis – summer **c)** project – jobs – kindergarten – motor – jockey – farmers – World Cup **d)** monster – sand – character – film **e)** bank – computer **f)** kings – King – Great **g)** Queen Mother – Queen – mother › Seite 51

34. a) sweatshirt b) blackboard c) post office d) holidaymaker e) cake factory f) Christmas party g) own goal h) cricket match › Seite 52

35.
a) There are lots of holidaymakers in the Black Forest in the summer holidays.
b) In the last football match Fabian scored an own goal.
c) Stephen and Toby are going to stay in a youth hostel and do a sightseeing tour of London.
d) They're packing sweatshirts and pullovers in their rucksacks.
e) There's a school trip so there are lots of schoolchildren at the main entrance of the school.
f) The school bus is taking them to the railway station.
g) Toby is a vegetarian so he won't be eating bacon sandwiches and hot dogs like his classmates.
h) They will be travelling on the underground.
i) How does the ticket machine work?

36. a) 2; b) 2; c) 2; d) 1; e) 2; f) 1; g) 2; h) 3; i) 2; j) 2; k) 1 › Seite 53

37. a) Castle Tennis Club b) Dave's Café c) Beach Hotel d) 3 o'clock Bar e) All Saints' Church f) Anne's Cheese Shop g) Tom's Taxis

38. rugby, jewel; correct; autumn; design; divorced; doctor; about; slogan; little; mustn't; careful; › Seite 54

39. a) Asia b) shelter c) driver d) camera e) motor f) smuggler g) metre h) visitor i) actor j) figure k) popular l) either m) adventure n) calendar

40. a) delicious b) nervous c) actress d) dangerous e) religious f) famous g) waitress

41. present; restaurant; brilliant, elephant; assistant; accident; important; parent; different; pavement

42. a) Have you heard the stupid story of the ghost rabbit in the haunted house opposite the cricket ground?
b) jacket; favourite; packet; hundred; helmet; toilet; ticket; supermarket › Seite 55

43. a) discuss b) describe c) detective d) divorced e) discussion f) disabled g) delicious h) decide i) disappear j) design

44. a) across b) assistant c) opinion d) until

45. a) assistant b) across c) ago d) appear e) adventure f) against g) around h) arrive i) above j) agree k) address l) abroad m) assembly; Der Eindringling ist ein **r**.

46. a) Bob; b) Harry: hero – disco; Phil: window; c) Phil › Seite 56

47. a) ex- b) re- c) com- d) ex- e) to- f) un- g) pre- h) re- i) to- j) com- k) ex- l) un-
Die Eindringlinge sind *con-* und *per-*.

48. a) -ic b) -age c) -ful d) -ive e) -ish f) -ic g) -ice h) -age i) -ic j) -ful k) -ish l) -age
Die beiden Irrläufer sind *-tion* und *-er*. › Seite 57

49. Some of Mr Norton's pupils travel to school by bus. Others cycle. The school is quite near the hospital.

50. a) apple b) April c) little d) candle e) people f) animal g) bicycle h) whistle i) uncle › Seite 58

51. hostel – magical – smuggler – bicycle – travel – castle – candle – central – classical – label – bottle – table – traditional – meal – festival – unusual – jewellery – real – little – people – beautiful;
Das Lösungswort: double trouble!

Seite 59 ❮

52. a) engine b) given c) conversation d) bacon e) forgotten f) happen
g) expression h) European i) Asian j) kitchen k) Indian l) open

Seite 60 ❮

53. a) budgie b) hockey c) empty d) dictionary e) coffee f) taxi
g) journey h) Sunday i) maybe

54. Es gibt 13 Stellen, wo stumme Konsonanten vorkommen:
-gh- (daughter); -s- (island); -t- (castle); -l- (walks); -l- (talk); -l- (could); -h- und -t- (whistle); k- (knew); -l- (shouldn't); -gh- (night); -n (autumn); k- (knock);

Seite 61 ❮

55. everybody; queue; suitable; fruit; biscuit; dialogue; frightening; national; Übrig bleibt **i**.

56. bone – south – soon – supermarket – alone – unit; forest – below – actor; mean – even; study – young; both – above – south; tour – sure – dear; dialogue; repeat – skiing; ago – manage – language

A woman woke her husband up and said, "there's a man in the kitchen. He's eating the biscuits I made today. Phone the emergency services!"
"Who shall I ask for?" said her husband, "police or ambulance?"

Seite 62 ❮

57. a) kiss – house b) famous – religious c) scientist d) entrance
e) glass – dangerous f) divorced g) else h) ambulance
i) horse – nervous j) false – exercises
Joke: Ann and Becky … "… five hundred thousand ants CAN'T have MADE a MISTAKE."

Seite 63 ❮

58. watching – match – exchanging – chart – cheese – kitchen – reach – much – church – Which – choose

59. Dear Jane,
Thank you for your letter. My **English** isn't very good, I have to use a **dictionary** for lots of words and **expressions**. But I'm **sure** I **shall** improve. You say that you like **traditional** **Asian** foods like rice and **fish**. I do, too, but my mother says I eat too much **sugar**. **She** says I'm getting fat. My favourite food is chocolate ice cream. **Delicious**! Is it true that the **national** sport of the **British** people is football? I must **finish** now. Best **wishes** to you and your parents, Love, Mao.

Seite 64 ❮

60. a) for example b) exercise c) exchange d) taxi
e) exciting f) explain g) accident h) next

61. a) autumn – Christmas – concert
b) office – entrance – corridor
c) languages – German
d) organizing – mountains – forests
e) airport – vegetarian – pilot
f) souvenir – tourists – usually
g) cupboards – favourite – opposite

Seite 65 ❮

62.

N	R	W	T	E	O	Z	S	Y	B	J	C	A	Y	P	J	K	Q
O	Q	A	U	T	U	M	N	M	I	B	O	A	U	E	M	Y	K
E	F	H	O	Q	A	M	I	U	J	X	I	Z	S	A	I	C	V
P	B	W	T	Y	C	L	I	M	B	A	Y	U	W	T	S	R	D
L	T	H	D	B	C	I	K	F	N	C	X	G	Y	F	L	W	I
K	N	O	W	B	S	C	X	T	B	F	N	A	B	B	A	E	X
N	Z	N	A	J	O	H	D	V	R	I	Q	D	R	E	N	N	L
J	G	F	L	N	I	R	K	M	E	W	S	P	L	L	D	F	W
B	H	W	K	S	G	I	X	E	V	H	P	C	V	L	J	D	R
A	X	X	A	H	S	S	S	A	E	I	K	U	U	Z	R	L	I
N	T	C	M	S	O	T	X	G	R	E	H	Q	F	I	V	Z	T
V	D	L	W	I	H	M	V	D	Y	Q	W	H	I	S	T	L	E
H	H	L	H	G	I	A	M	U	W	H	G	A	A	I	N	J	U
B	M	P	I	N	K	S	D	Z	H	Y	D	Q	U	L	Y	U	R
E	L	S	R	S	Z	J	C	G	E	Q	E	R	O	Q	V	V	V
T	R	T	K	P	T	S	K	W	R	S	F	M	F	E	O	E	Z
O	P	G	G	W	E	E	Q	U	E	U	E	K	S	O	A	C	S
L	T	S	C	C	N	I	N	T	K	C	Q	P	G	G	U	F	B

E Words in context 2

1. adverts – UK – lazily – peaceful – canals – control – difficult – Isles – fields – although – Skybus – passengers – escape – crowds – cows – Welsh – harbours - nature › Seite 77
2. lazy › Seite 78
3. Isles
4. peaceful; fields
5. cows; crowds
6. a) peace: ▼ piece: ◇
   b) piece – peace(ful) – peace – piece(s)
7. a) although; also; b) although: △ also: ◆ c) although – although – also
8. They like FOREIGN ones. › Seite 79
9. • Spanish – choice – instruction – grammar – barbecues – experience • Canyon – yourself • wondering – might – especially – neighbours
10. Spanish – instruction – especially › Seite 80
11. a) spend: ✻ spent: ⌘ b) spent – spend – spend – spent
12. a) we're: ▼ wear: ▲ where: ◆ b) Where – We're – wear – where – wear
13. a) board: ◁ bored: ▷ b) bored – board – board – board(ing) › Seite 81
14. Are you going to be at the barbecue?
15. success – square – such – covered – snow – drained – bottom – since – successful – industry – expect – busiest – attitudes – role › Seite 82
16. attitude; busy; drain; cover
17. success – successful – expect
18. a) its: ◇ it's: ⌕ b) its – it's – it's › Seite 83
19. COTTON
20. touch – taste – gifts – volunteers – engineers - support – businesses – exciting – such – marriage
21. a) his: ◆ he's: □ b) He's – his – his – He's – his › Seite 84
22. a) hour: ▲ our: ▼ hours: ▽ ours: ◇ b) Our – hour – ours – hours
23. PINEAPPLE (Ananas) › Seite 85
24. definitely – foreign – business – spices – mention – route – vehicles – robbed – thieves – enemies – attacked – continue
25. attack; vehicle; rob; spice; enemy; thief › Seite 86
26. foreign – vehicle
27. bestimmt – definitely; ausländisch – foreign; Gewürze – spices; Dieb – thief; fortsetzen – continue
28. a) there: ▲ their: ◆ they're: ✻; b) their – They're – there – their – They're – their
29. a) knows: ▲ nose: ◆; b) nose – nose – knows – knows – nose › Seite 87
30. attack – definitely – continue – foreign – business – enemy
    Marco Polo … passed through HORMUZ …
31. Fortunately – died – palace – belonged – Chinese – celebrations – spoons – caught – prison – While – journeys – famous › Seite 88
32. catch; die
33. famous; palace
34. celebration; prison; fortunately; journeys; Chinese

Seite 89 ❮ 35. **a)** by: ▶ buy: ◆ **b)** buy – by – by – by

36. believed – edge – arguments – death – similar – argued – Christian – secret – alive – disagreed – executed

37. argue; execute; disagree; believe

Seite 90 ❮ 38. c) fifteen forty-three

39. **a)** edge **b)** alive **c)** secret **d)** similar

40. **a)** of: ▽ off: ▷; **b)** off – of – off – of – of – of – of

41. Copernicus was born in POLAND.

Seite 91 ❮ 42. mysteries – education – communication – news – catalogues – contact – chess – cable – techniques – surgery – surgeon – control – heart

43. *heart* wird anders ausgesprochen. Es reimt sich mit *part*.

44. catalogue; technique; mystery

Seite 92 ❮ 45. **a)** through: ▼ threw: ▽ **b)** through – threw

46. It took two and a half WEEKS for the news to reach London.

Seite 93 ❮ 47. communications – experience – differences – coins – purses – moon – survey – space – requests – really – unless – spare

48. difference; purse

49. **a)** spare **b)** request **c)** survey **d)** experience

50. **a)** blau: how; du: who; **b)** how: ◀ who: ▷ **c)** who – Who – How – How

Seite 94 ❮ 51. CABLE **G**UITAR BRAIN **A**RROW EXECUTE **G**RAFFITI CHESS **A**STRONAUT CELEBRATE **R**EQUEST OPERATE **I**NDUSTRY UNLESS **N**EWS **GAGARIN**

52. people – nationalities – graffiti – messages – hurt – worry – popular – choose – term – voted – properly – politely – opinions

Seite 95 ❮ 53. vote

54. nationality

55. **a)** keys – these; kiss – this
b) **this** … sweatshirt – farmer – address – detective – money – bag of sweets
these – easy questions – trousers – shoes – people – funny mice
c) this: ◇ these: □
d) this – these – this – these

Seite 96 ❮ 56. windsurfing

57. miserable – hates – real – since – celebrating – barbecue – including – mostly – mirrors – themselves – perfumes – anyway – fat

Seite 97 ❮ 58. celebrating – themselves – anyway

59. barbecue – perfumes

60. hate; perfume; include; celebrate

61. **a)** know: ▷ no: ◁ **b)** know – no – No – know

62. Joanna is a CLEVER girl. echt – *real*; elend – *miserable*; sie sich – *themselves*; Grillfest – *barbecue*; Spiegel – *mirror*

Seite 98 ❮ 63. tears – positive – mood – cheer – guitar – plug – operate – coal – fridge – oven – sugar – arrows – poems – success

64. [ɒ] (wie in *got*): operate [ʌ] (wie in *bus*): oven

65. dear: tear; you'd: mood; role: coal

Seite 99 ❮ 66. **a)** see: ▼ sea: ▲ **b)** see – sea – see – see – sea

67. Linda was miserable at first, but cheered up when she played with the others. Later she danced with Peter and knew she was happy.

F Word workshop 2

1. a) crisps b) churches c) lakes d) moves e) agrees f) classes › Seite 100
g) matches h) dialogues

2. a) dictionary b) factory c) carry d) journey e) wife f) shelf

3. a) A **car** ✓ is a four-wheeled **vehicle** ✓ …
b) Two hundred **years** ago … no **cars**, … **vehicles**
c) … **fairies**? Jasmin **believes** in them, … **brothers** don't.
d) The **park** ✓ … **trees** and **paths**. … a **place** ✓ … a **fairy** ✓ … **lives**
e) If anyone **touches** …, it **runs** away. … **run** ✓ … Andy **touches** … **hamsters**
f) … a **business** ✓ trip, he found six **faxes** and …

4. a) The **buskers** … play nice **music** ✓ › Seite 101
b) Fabian always **hurries** to **catch** ✓ … Paul doesn't **hurry** ✓; he usually gets up and **goes** …
c) Lots of **businesses** and art **galleries** produce **catalogues** …
d) In Britain the **railways** are being repaired, so the **trains** … on long **journeys** can **expect** ✓ to **arrive** ✓ between one and two **hours** late.
e) Although the **trains** are often late, the **buses** usually run on time.
f) In English, you usually **start** ✓ a speech … **Ladies** and gentlemen …

5. a) **Life** ✓ in the country … **life** ✓ in a big **city** ✓
b) Jane … the **lives** of the great **composers** …
c) The **police** ✓ have posters … there's a **thief** ✓ …
d) … a lot of **thieves** who **climb** ✓ in through **windows** and take expensive **jewellery** ✓ and other **things**.
e) If there are **visitors** there, … Did you make it **yourself** ✓ ?
f) … 'You'll have to look after **yourselves** this evening.'

6. controlled – panicked – celebrated – drained – argued – attacked – robbed – chased – plugged – pulled – pushed – travelled – added – visited › Seite 102

7. cry – **die** – try

8. a) counted b) robbed c) attacked d) supported e) visited › Seite 103
f) celebrated g) killed – shocked h) plugged i) scanned

9. a) lose – lost b) find – found c) built – build d) understood – understand
e) read – read f) held – hold

10. learning – learn; practising – practise; Stopping – stop; falling – fall; Skiing – ski; getting – get; driving – drive; lying – lie; having – have; trying – try; finding – find › Seite 104

11. In the kitchen: taste – eat; In the living room: sit – break; Upstairs: lie – wake up › Seite 105

12. dying – arguing – robbing – controlling – covering – disagreeing › Seite 106

13. a) arranging b) carrying c) tying d) escaping e) fixing f) offering
g) travelling h) panicking i) plugging j) scanning k) snowing

14. a) noisy b) fat c) small d) wide

15. a) crazier b) laziest c) strictest d) strongest e) strangest f) gladder › Seite 107
g) richest h) politer

16. a) lucky b) real c) sudden d) wonderful › Seite 108

17. a) terrible b) expensive c) horrible d) fine
e) Alle Grundformen enden mit dem Buchstaben **-e**
f) Die Regel heißt richtig: Bei Adjektiven, die mit *-able* / *-ible* enden, wird bei der Bildung des Adverbs das End-e **weggelassen.** Das „*l*“ der Grundform **bleibt als Einzelkonsonant**.
g) miserable – **miserably**

18. **lazily**; defin**itely**; especially; really; fortu**nately**; exactly; pat**iently**; success**fully**; Die Insel heißt ATLANTIS.

19. thief's; can't; lady's; won't; there's › Seite 109

Seite 109 ‹

20. Karen; London; Christian; Italy; American; etc.; skiing; winter; today

21. … **We've** moved in … **Mr** and Mrs **Stone** … the **neighbours'** dishes … I think **we're** getting … **it's** not in the garage … borrowing **Stephen's** … he **won't** want … nice, **it's** a bit … especially **Mrs** Brice … for **Maths** and Physics … from **Wolstanton**, … Boulton **Street**, … an **Indian** girl … an **English** name … celebrate **Christian** festivals as **they're** **Hindus** … works on **Christmas Day** … for a **London** … called **Cheetah Transport**. … Oak **Tree** Road … **You've** got … **I've** got.
Großbuchstaben: 16:4 = 4 Fehlende Apostrophe: 10

Seite 111 ‹

22. **One word**: microphone, doorbell, centimetre, grandparents, although, railway, ourselves, himself, homeless, anyway
Lösung: *kettledrum* (Pauke)
Der Rest sind zwei Wörter. Lösung: *French horn* (Waldhorn)

Seite 112 ‹

23. National Gallery; Foreign Office; Government Communications Headquarters; Public Library; Buckingham Palace; Passport Control; Strangeways Prison; Unbenutzte Buchstaben: MILK

24. a) enemies b) volunteer c) guitar d) bottom e) role
Übrig bleiben die Buchstaben für AUTUMN.

Seite 113 ‹

25. support; attitude; supposed; graffiti; difficult; passenger;
Lösungswort: The PUPILS won.

26. Isles; autumn; although; foreign; neighbour; vehicle; unknown

27. guitar; fridge; biscuit; mystery; since; religion; strict; symbol; rich; busy; disagree; business; similar; miserable; übrig bleibt: i

28. Die Wörter mit [i:]: graffiti; field; police; technique; vehicle
Das Lösungswort: CHINA.

Seite 114 ‹

29. Die Lautkombination [ju:] kommt bei „Hindu" und „Urdu" nicht vor.

30. Asian elephant

31. **Unverändert:** astronaut; route; parade; pause; planet; religion; symbol; motor; person
Mit einem -e dazu: nature; negative; positive; relative; type
Ohne End-e: attack; legend; period; sandal

Seite 115 ‹

32. a)

action	Oo;	control	oO
contact	Oo	planet	Oo
guitar	oO	legend	Oo
nature	Oo	patient	Oo
sandal	Oo	perfume	Oo

b)

vehicle	Ooo	technique	oO
passenger	Ooo	miserable	Ooo
gallery	Ooo	direction	oOo
biology	oOoo	difference	Oo
period	Ooo		

33. Christian; busker; cable; Christmas; character; electronic; panic; technique

34. accident; expect; escape; execution; especially; successful;
The biggest lake in the world is in CANADA.

Seite 116 ‹

35. Die Wörter ohne [z] sind: conversation; expensive; December. Lösunswort: BAT.

36. business; crazy; example; Muslim; prison; lazy; easier; noisy; suppose; exactly
What did the man do? He MOVED HOUSE. (Er zog um.)

Seite 117 ‹

37. Mit -ti-: action; communication; instruction; mention; patient.
Mit -sh: push; flash; Spanish; Welsh.
Mit anderen Buchstaben: sugar; discussion; especially; delicious; sure; Asian.
Die Lösungswörter: JAMES DEAN; (Humphrey) BOGART

38. smell; such; astronaut; success; phrase; replace; Muslim; space; nose

› *Seite 118*

39.

experience	based (on)
passenger	peaceful
since	spicy
successful	celebrate
replace	secret
purse	choice
	escape
	space

40. Die Wörter, die sich unterscheiden: homeless – **palace** – business; famous – delicious – **helpless**; **waitress** – nervous – dangerous

› *Seite 119*

41. Die vollständigen Wörter: **a)** harbour (14); **b)** enter (17); **c)** doctor (15); **d)** grammar (9); **e)** sugar (15); **f)** centimetre (7); **g)** offer (120); **h)** busker (122); **i)** operator (10); **j)** dollar (17); **k)** mirror (55); **l)** neighbour (69); **m)** similar (34)